Troopships to Calais

CALAIS 2

PCR IR/2

BASSIN CARNOT

AVANT PORT DE L'EST

AVANT PORT DE L'OUEST

BASSIN DU PARADIS

BASSIN A FLOT DE L'OUEST

JETÉE OUEST

(a) Time Zone Zone.
(b) L.A.T. Datum (1¾ inches)

TROOPSHIPS TO CALAIS

The story of Calais as a military port
from 1944 to 1947 and the ships which served it.

by
Derek Spiers

For B & D

Published for the author by
MERESBOROUGH BOOKS

Published for the author by Meresborough Books, 17 Station Road, Rainham, Kent. ME8 7RS.

Meresborough Books is a specialist publisher of books about Kent. A list of publications currently available will be found at the back of this book.

ISBN 0948193 395

Printed and bound in Great Britain by Mackays of Chatham PLC, Chatham, Kent

CONTENTS

Foreword

When invited by the author, Major (he was promoted to this rank when he left Calais for 21st Army Group HQ in March 1946) Derek Spiers, to write a Foreword, I said I would be only too pleased to do so, having been involved in this story right from the start following my appointment as Port Commandant of Calais by HQ 21st Army Group on 2nd October, 1944.

The story also shows the value of the training at the Combined Operations School in Inveraray (the first course of which I attended on 1st January, 1942). The result was that the Royal Navy, including Sea Transport, plus the Mercantile Marine, the Army and Royal Air Force (Movements) worked together as a team in Calais from the start with great success and friendliness. Any problems were thrashed out in committees. The French civil authorities under Jacques Vendroux (General de Gaulle's brother-in-law), Liberation Mayor of Calais, provided civilian labour for the construction of the transit camps and also cooking and cleaning staff once they were built. The Calais port officials (Ponts et Chaussees) were also involved in the reconstruction of the dock area. The co-operation of all concerned enabled us to meet the deadlines set by HQ, 21st Army Group for the movement of troops, vehicles and locomotives.

We also worked in close harmony with my old friend the late Lt. Col. Cedric Aldworth, M.C., Port Commandant of Dover/Folkestone and his colleagues both in the Army and other services, not forgetting H.M. Customs under 'Steve' Steadman, still living in Dover, who helped to speed up disembarkation in the U.K.

Derek Spiers, as one of my staff officers, played a leading part in, the planning of this vast movement of personnel. He was partly motivated by his great interest in the passenger ships. This enabled him to tell the name of a ship at least 5 miles away by recognising the set of the ship's funnel(s) and masts(s). I suspect he would often have preferred to be down on the quay rather than in the office. But this enthusiasm and knowledge has enabled him to produce a story with vivid descriptions and accurate detail.

G.H.W. Wharton, OBE, Croix de Guerre
Lieutenant Colonel

Acknowledgements

The author acknowledges with thanks the co-operation of the Public Record Office at Kew, Mr Alan Pearsall and his colleagues at the National Maritime Museum, Greenwich, the Photographic and Research Departments of the Imperial War Museum and the Ministry of Defence (Army and Naval Historical Branches). Unfortunately the records of the Naval and Sea Transport contingents stationed in Calais appear to have been destroyed. Mr John Edgington of the National Railway Museum, York, gave me access to the unique Southern Railway collection of photographs. The Editors of the 'Dover Express' and 'Folkestone Herald' made backnumbers of their papers available.

On the personal side I am grateful to John Hendy for shipping advice and to him and the late David Nye for their help and encouragement. I am also indebted to the following: Captain G.D. Walker, D.S.C., who, at the age of 91, corrected my draft chapter on the *Canterbury*, Captain John Arthur, retired Commodore of Sealink U.K., for his contribution on the Train Ferries and Mr Henry Maxwell for his assistance on Southern Railway ships.

From the Isle of Man, Richard Danielson lent me photographs while Mr Shimmon and Mr Speers of the Isle of Man Steam Packet Company and Captains McMeikin and Griffin, former Masters, provided information. John Pover, retired Chief Engineer of the P & O Steam Navigation Company helped with *Royal Daffodil* and *Laird's Isle* while Mrs E. Iles sent me the obituary of her late husband, Captain S. Iles, Master of the *Princess Maud*.

Among my former Army colleagues Lieutenant Colonel George Wharton read the Army chapters, Captain Tony Griffiths took the bulk of the photographs of the ships in Calais whilst the photographs of the *Invicta* and *Dinard* in Dover were given to me by the late Major A.W. Hallifax. An old friend, Derrick Croxon, reproduced the Imperial War Museum pictures of Calais in 1944.

Sir Peter Allen and John de S. Winter also kindly provided photographs as did Keith Lewis and John Clarkson.

Finally, my grateful thanks go to Miss Myrtle Correya who patiently typed the manuscript.

Introduction

I arrived in Calais on 27th December, 1944 and left on 15th March, 1946. This was by far the longest time I ever spent in one place during my 5½ years Army service. This book is in no sense an autobiography, but a little background is necessary to explain why so much of it is devoted to the ships and how I came to be in Calais.

I grew up as a boy in Kent where my father had coal and shipping interests on the Medway. As a result I spent much of my summer holidays on the 15 odd paddle (and from 1935 diesel) pleasure steamers in the Thames Estuary. Dover and Folkestone were also within easy reach and my interest in the cross channel scene thus dates back to the 1930s. I crossed the Straits four times before the war, twice through Boulogne and twice through Ostend but not through Calais.

Dover and Folkestone were to become familiar again in 1942 when I was stationed successively in both ports as a subaltern in The Buffs (Royal East Kent Regiment). But there were, of course, no cross channel ships there at that time.

In view of my nautical interests I suppose I was lucky to arrive in Egypt, in the spring of 1943, when the Beach Bricks were being formed for the Mediterranean invasions. These special units — those formed in the U.K. were known as Beach *Groups* — comprised a force about 3,000 strong of all branches of the Army. They landed with the leading brigades of the assault divisions to consolidate the beachhead and develop the lodgement area through which the assaulting troops could pass inland. In this capacity I landed with 35 Beach Brick at Salerno and with 36 Beach Brick in Normandy. We were, I think, the only Beach unit kept intact for further emergency landings but, after Arromanches, acted as Garrison Headquarters and provided troops in various roles to assist in opening up the ports of Boulogne and, subsequently, Calais.

The rapid expansion of the latter port found the Q (Movements) pool short of officers and I was quite happy to be transferred to the Port Commandant's staff together with about 20 of my fellow officers.

What happened after that will become clear in the book.

9

Calais: the Dock Area showing bombing by R.A.F. in September 1944. Calais Nord was destroyed by the Germans in 1940. Entrance Channel and Quai Gare Maritime on left.

(Imperial War Museum)

PART I

Chapter I
The Liberation of Calais

'Calais was invested . . . and fell on 30th September'
Churchill

Airey Neave has described in his book 'The Flames of Calais' the epic defence of the Port in May 1940 by the Rifle Brigade, the King's Royal Rifle Corps, the Queen Victoria's Rifles, the Royal Tank Regiment and other units.

The recapture of Calais, Boulogne and the area around Cap Gris Nez, where the heavy cross channel guns were sited, was entrusted to the 2nd Canadian Corps and largely undertaken by the 3rd Canadian Division. Boulogne, which had the larger and tougher German garrison, surrendered on 22nd September, 1944 and over 9,000 prisoners were taken. Following this a two pronged attack (Operation 'UNDERGO') was mounted in conjunction with the R.A.F. on the outer defences of Calais and Cap Gris Nez.

The softening up process from the air was considerable. Over 3,000 tons of bombs were dropped on the Calais defences on 20th September. The Germans put up an active resistance and seven bombers were lost.

By 26th September, the outlying villages surrounding Calais of Coquelles, Escalles and Sangatte had all been captured. The G.O.C. 3rd Canadian Infantry Division, Major General Spry, ordered 7th Brigade (Regina Rifle Regiment, Royal Winnipeg Rifles and 1st Canadian Scottish Regiment) to attack from the West (Sangatte) and south towards Calais Sud and the factory area. 8th Brigade (Queens Own Rifles of Canada, Cameron Highlanders of Ottawa) and 7th Reconnaissance Regiment would attack from the south east while 9th Brigade cleared up the Cap Gris Nez area. This latter operation was completed on 29th September, though before then on 26th September the Germans, to use up their ammunition, had subjected the Dover area to a heavy bombardment. 1,600 prisoners were taken in this area.

The main attack on the Calais perimeter began on 28th September preceded by heavy bombing. Progress was made but the Canadians suffered casualties from shellfire, mines and obstructions. A truce was agreed for 29th September to permit the evacuation of 10,000 French civilians. The German Commander (Lt. Col. Schroeder) indicated that he did not wish to continue to fight but had been ordered to do so by Hitler.

Hostilities therefore recommenced at noon on 30th September. By 1500 hours the enemy were surrendering in large numbers. By midnight resistance ceased with the capture of the German Commander and mopping up operations were completed by 0900 hours on 1st October. 7,500 prisoners were captured. Canadian casualties were under 300 of which 190 were suffered by 7th Brigade.

General Spry in a message to his Division said that they brought safety and peace to Dover and Folkestone and would, in the future, be glad to say 'I was there'.

Quai Gare Maritime in 1928, showing hotel and pre-war station. The Prince of Wales (subsequently Edward VIII) has disembarked from the British destroyer alongside.

Chapter 2
The Reconstruction of the Port

The Canadians' initial report was that the town was in a bad shape with much debris blocking roads and one main axis open to the centre. But this referred largely to Calais Sud i.e., the area from the Hotel de Ville to the Place du Theatre. Calais Nord, which comprises the main dock area, had been flattened in 1940; no rebuilding had been undertaken and much of it was still mined. We are really only concerned with the Port area (see map). The Avant Port and Quai Gare Maritime and harbour entrance lie to the north east of the town, the Bassin Carnot to the east and the Bassin de l'Ouest to the north west.

Naval

The initial work in the harbour was done by the Royal Navy assisted by the U.S. Navy. They found the harbour entrance mined and obstructed by nets and six small vessels sunk as block ships. Controlled minefields were located and eight other mines could be hauled ashore. Four moored mines were sunk by gunfire. Despite the block ships a channel 70' wide existed in the centre. By 11th October an approach channel had been opened and the sweeping of the Avant Port completed. The block ships were largely lifted rather than dispersed by explosives. By 29th October a channel 120' wide (extended to 250' by 15th November) and 25' – 28' deep had been cleared. The U.S. Naval Party were withdrawn at the end of October. The Senior Royal Naval officer (Commander Freemantle) was upgraded to N.O.I.C. (Naval Officer in Charge) on 6th November and to SNOBOP(F) (Senior Naval Officer British Occupied Ports France) on 1st January, 1945, reporting to the Admiral commanding Dover.

Army

Army reconstruction work did not commence until 22nd October as the port was initially offered to the U.S. authorities on 5th October. This would however have cut across the British and Canadian lines of communication and the offer was declined on 19th October.

Quai Gare Maritime in 1937. *Canterbury* and *Queen of the Channel* are alongside.

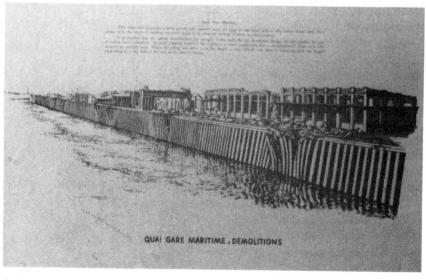

Quai Gare Maritime showing demolitions in 1944.   (Imperial War Museum)

14

The British moved swiftly after this. Lt. Col. George Wharton, O.B.E., Croix de Guerre, accompanied by his Staff Captain, John Walker, had already arrived. Lt. Col. Wharton, who had participated in the landings in North Africa, Sicily, Salerno and Normandy, was to remain as Port Commandant for 18 months. He had been earmarked as Port Commandant of Rotterdam but, since this huge port was not liberated until the end of the war, the Army made very limited use of it as distinct from the Hook of Holland.

The immediate formidable task was the repair of the quays and access routes. This was initially entrusted to No.2 Port Construction and Repair Group, (Lt. Col. C.P. Shelbourne, O.B.E., G.M.) with 934, 935, 936 and 937 P.C. & R. Companies under command assisted by 44 Mechanical Engineering (Tn) Section and 983 Dredging Companies. The first priorities were the construction of a Train Ferry terminal at the landward end of the Quai Gare Maritime by the entrance to the Bassin Carnot and of Landing Ships Tank hards at the landward end of the Quai Paul Devot, the other side of the entrance to the Bassin Carnot and opposite the Quai Gare Maritime. A detailed account of the work undertaken is outside the scope of this book but an excellent record complete with photos and drawings can be found in the Imperial War Museum*. Some of the pictures are reproduced here.

Suffice it to say that the Train Ferry Berth was completed by 15th November, one L.S.T. hard by 27th November and a second by 20th December.

High priority was also given to the Quai Gare Maritime to receive the personnel ships and the Quai Paul Devot where coasters and particularly Army mail ships were to berth.

To anyone who knew the Gare Maritime at Calais before the war, with its imposing hotel above the station, the area was unrecognisable. The buildings were in ruins, 120' wide craters pitted the quay at regular intervals, railway lines had been torn up and access roads cratered.

The quay itself had been faced by the French Pont et Chaussées with heavy section steel sheeting in 1937. Demolition charges did not produce the size of damage found elsewhere; but, where piling had burst, it was difficult to trim back because of jagged projections. The

---

* 21 Army Group Port Repair Works by Transportation Units of the Royal Engineers — Dieppe, Boulogne and Calais.

TRAIN FERRY TERMINAL.

Quai Gare Maritime — construction of Train Ferry Berth.   (Imperial War Museum)

Army's answer was to build a line of vertical steel fenders ('dolphins') backed by timber 6'6" in front of the old quay wall. The solution was not ideal as all the cross channel ships involved were used to a solid quay wall and had protruding rubbing strakes. This produced pressure on a single fender when berthing in a westerly wind. However by 23rd December, 1944 the first personnel ship (the *Canterbury*) was accepted for berthing trials. By April 1945, three berths were available and sets of steel box piles were replacing the initial temporary repairs. The craters were filled in and temporary roofing of the Gare Maritime provided some shelter for troops waiting to embark.

The Train Ferry berth presented special problems but the three ships concerned had had overhead gantries fitted at the stern which enabled them to load and unload their engines and waggons. The first ship to undergo berthing trials (the *Shepperton Ferry*) brought over a ramp so that vehicles could drive on and off. A rail track was already in position by then to receive engines, coaches and waggons. The pre-war Train Ferry dock at the town end of the Bassin Carnot had been destroyed.

Canterbury on berthing trials, 23rd December 1944.

Once the initial military priorities had been met, the units concerned were able to concentrate, in conjunction with the French authorities, on the main freight dock area, the Bassin Carnot. As the lock gates had been destroyed, this was initially tidal but a 'shark' unit was floated into position by May 1945. This kept the water in the dock but could be lowered to the sea bed at high tides to allow the passage of ships in and out. The trickle of much needed imports into France which had been taking place at the tidal berths was thus materially increased. Repairs were also made to the Bassin de l'Ouest.

It is a tribute to the devoted work of the British service personnel and the French port authorities that major damage was sustained by only one ship (see *Princess Astrid*) during the military tenure of the port.

Boulogne in November 1944. The top photograph shows the demolished Quai Gare Maritime on the left.

18

Chapter 3
The Organisation and Build Up of the Port

1 The need for Calais

The decision by SHAEF (Supreme Headquarters Allied Expedition-
ary Forces) and 21st Army Group HQ (then in Brussels) to make
Calais the main personnel port for 21st Army Group (2nd British
Army and 1st Canadian Army) was not taken until 18th December,
1944. The position regarding other ports in the autumn and winter of
1944, which led to this decision, was:

(a) 21st Army Group

DIEPPE
The town was, rightly, in view of their 1942 raid, liberated by the
Canadians without a struggle on 4th September, 1944. Despite the
destruction of the lock gates which made the inner port tidal, the port
was fully operational by mid September when up to 15 coastal supply
ships arrived and departed on each high tide. A Train Ferry berth for
the London and North Eastern Railway 'Zeebrugge' type ships (i.e.
not the three which were to use Calais) was in use by 29th September.
Personnel berths and rail communications except to Paris were, however, limited.

BOULOGNE
Liberated on 22nd September, 1944, this was the most heavily
damaged of all the ports due to effective demolition by a tenacious
garrison and bombing attacks by the Allies on the E-boat pens. In
particular the Quai Gare Maritime was completely destroyed (see picture) and therefore useless for personnel until July, 1947. However,
limited capacity for Landing Craft Tanks and cargo ships was
available by 12th October. On 24th October, the coaster *Guernsey
Queen* was blown up by a delayed action mine, blocking the entrance
to the Bassin à Flot and trapping four ships inside the dock. The port
was handed back to the French in January, 1945 though a small
number of hospital ships berthed opposite the Quai Gare Maritime
after that date.

Calais on 15th February 1946. Private Neale (4 millionth man to pass through Calais) is being greeted by Captain Woods, Master of the *Lady of Mann*.   (Imperial War Museum)

OSTEND

This port was captured without a struggle in the first week of September, 1944. Repair work started on 14th September and the first ship was received on 29th September. Damage was not as extensive as at some ports and the Quai Gare Maritime was able to receive the first personnel ship on 7th December. Ostend was essentially a 'duty' port receiving ships from Dover and Tilbury. While the war lasted it had the disadvantage of being closer to German E-boats and midget submarines operating from Dutch bases. A Landing Ship Tank and two supply ships were sunk off the port.

ANTWERP

Following its surprising capture on 4th September, it was promptly designated as the main British/Canadian supply base but, because the Germans were not driven from the Scheldt estuary until November, it was not operational until the 28th of that month. It suffered periodic attacks from V1s and V2s.

DUNKIRK

This was designated by Hitler like most other ports as a 'Fortress'. In view of the 1940 damage it was 'masked', i.e. contained, by 21st Army Group and not liberated until V.E. day although the bulk of the civilians were evacuated after the capture of Calais.

(b) U.S. 12th Army Group

LE HAVRE

This vast port was captured by the British on 12th September but was handed over to the U.S. forces. Extensive damage meant that the first ship was not received until 9th October and capacity never reached that of Antwerp, though large supply vessels and ships with U.S. personnel made increasing use of the port. Rouen was also opened up as a subsidiary cargo port.

CHERBOURG

Although far from the front, Cherbourg continued to be worked to capacity, almost entirely by U.S. forces, once Antwerp was operational. Other ports in Normandy, Brittany and Western and Southern France were also used by the Americans.

2 Policy Considerations

The decision on Calais was taken during the Ardennes offensive but the planners had to take account of both immediate and post-war factors. The Navy were decisively in favour of Calais because of the shortness of the crossing. The greater distance from the German Coastal forces meant that a protective screen could be provided further east and eliminated the need for organised convoys.

However, the planners also had in mind that a rail link would be needed immediately after the war to transport troops on leave and demobilization from Italy and Austria. This was to start initially through Dieppe but from 1st July, 1945 became an increasing element at Calais as first the Hook of Holland in July, 1945 and then Cuxhaven in November, 1945 were brought into use for 21st Army Group.

3 The Build Up

The numbers passing through Calais built up from 2,000 in both directions (1st – 3rd January, 1945) to 6,000 (4th January – 28th

Field Marshal Montgomery in Calais on 10th March 1946 with (left to right) Lt. Col. Wharton, Port Commandant, Col. McAlister, Garrison Commander and Captain Duggan, Master of *Ben-My-Chree*. *Invicta* is in background. Monty had arrived by destroyer and left by the 'Rhine Army Special' for H.Q.B.A.O.R.

February, 1945), 9,000 from 1st March, 12,000 by 1st April and 15,000 from 1st June. At first all troops were proceeding on leave but, increasingly during the autumn of 1945, demobilization was taken over from Ostend which finally closed as a military port in March, 1946.

On the U.K. side, Harwich was used for the first two months in addition to Dover and Folkestone. But the crossing was long and there were dangers both from the enemy, while the war lasted, and the weather. For three weeks in April, 1945 one sailing was diverted to Newhaven while the second berth at Folkestone was being dredged. Thereafter all troops were embarked for Dover and Folkestone. The latter port was returned to civilian use in March, 1946 following which all troops went to Dover until Calais closed on 1st August, 1947.

During the peak period from April, 1945 to March, 1946 Calais handled more personnel than all the other ports in 21st Army Group combined and, by the time it closed, some five million troops had passed through the port.

22

To accommodate these vast numbers, transit camps, with sleeping accommodation and rail links, had to be built. The initial No.1 Camp was in a school at Triage, Calais Sud, but the main area was on waste land east of the Bassin Carnot. This was served by the rail link between the Gare Centrale and the Gare Maritime. Here was built No.2 Camp, headquarters of 112 Transit Camp, No.3 Camp for outward bound personnel, No.4 Camp for inward bound troops and, at a later date, No.5 Camp for the Women's Services. French civilian labour was recruited not only for construction of Nissen huts but, more particularly, to serve as cooks etc — which made the rations more appetizing. Accommodation was designed for 18,000 but, on one particularly bad night in October, 1945 due to cancellation of sailings because of gales, 23,000 transit troops were in Calais. The camp organisation was commanded by Lt. Col. T.D. (Robin) Hood, O.B.E., Royal Sussex Regiment. He, like many others, came from 36 (originally 35) Beach Brick which provided the initial Garrison Headquarters for Calais first under Colonel 'Jock' Ralston, O.B.E. and then Lt. Col. Chambers. When the Brick was disbanded in the summer of 1945, 25 Garrison under the command of Colonel Ronnie McAlister, O.B.E., Argyll and Sutherland Highlanders, who had commanded 32 Beach Brick in Sicily, took over.

To bring the above facts to life, perhaps I may describe a typical day in the winter of 1945/6 in my work as Staff Captain (Shipping) to the Port Commandant. Telexes came in overnight giving numbers due on trains from Italy (Milan) and Austria (Villach). At 1000 hrs a phone call to 21st Army Group HQ (now British Army of the Rhine) at Bad Oeynhausen confirmed the numbers coming from Germany. This was followed by a conference with Sea Transport (mostly RNR or RNVR officers controlling the movements of the ships for the Ministry of War Transport) to confirm the ships available for the next day. Personnel were then allocated to ships by destination zones. At 1500 hrs a three-way hook up by phone to my opposite numbers in Dover and the War Office confirmed the numbers embarking on each ship at Calais the next day so that they could organize the trains. They in turn told me of the numbers returning which were passed on to the rail side and the transit camps.

To ensure that personnel embarked on the correct ships, each man was given a coloured card on arrival at the Transit Camp which was collected at the ship's gangway as he embarked. He thus knew he was travelling on the 'red' 'green' or 'blue' ship. It also provided a check on numbers embarked. Phone calls between 'Port of Calais' and

'Port of Dover' were naturally incessant particularly when the weather went sour or a ship broke down.

Initially leave zones were divided into three areas in the U.K. but this was subsequently increased to seven. The plot became more complex with the advent of demobilization ('release') so that on a typical day — 2nd January, 1946 — the numbers embarked by categories were:

BAOR	Leave	1900
	Release	2535
CMF/BTA	Leave	500
	Release	1000
CMF/BTA	RAF	500
Canadian Repatriates		950

The aim was to have four ships and five or six sailings; sometimes there were only three ships but, unusually, on this particular day we had five ships available so they were lightly loaded. The *Invicta* sailed for Dover at 0900 and 1545 hrs, the *Prinses Astrid* made one crossing to Dover at 1015 arriving back at 1445, the *Royal Daffodil* left for Folkestone at 1045 returning at 1615, the *Lady of Mann* arrived from Dover at 1115, sailed at 1215 and returned at 1700. The *Canterbury* came in from Folkestone at 0945 and sailed at 1615.

Apart from the personnel in the Shipping Office at the Port Commandant's Headquarters opposite the Parc St Pierre near the Hôtel de Ville, there were of course a number of Embarkation Staff Officers, under an E.S.O.I.C. (to whom I had a direct line) and men working on the quays.

A similar operation prevailed on the rail side, though here there was more contact with other movements personnel in Western Europe and less with the U.K. Initially the railheads were in Belgium and the Netherlands, but, following the conclusion of the war, these were extended to the British Zone of Germany. By July, 1945 twenty trains ran to and from ten railheads in Germany, Belgium and the Netherlands. This month saw also the beginning of the long rail hauls from Villach (British Troops Austria) and Milan (Central Mediterranean Forces). The total number of trains in a 24 hour period was only four initially but increased later to twelve on these two routes.

In the autumn of 1945, when BAOR release commenced via Calais, a number of trains ran from Tournai in Belgium; this camp being the processing centre for BAOR demobilization.

The Train Ferries had brought over additional stock to cope with this movement particularly from Italy and Austria. No one can pretend that the conditions were luxurious and, especially on the Italian and Austrian routes, meal halts were necessary. Not unnaturally the spirits of those going to the U.K. were higher than of those returning.

The third element of the large Movements staff in Calais operated in the Transit Camps. Not only did this involve a series of broadcasts over powerful tannoys (loudspeakers) on the arrival and departure of each train. In addition travel enquiry offices were set up to deal with the innumerable queries. The Movements personnel were also in continuous liaison with the Transit Camp Staff over numbers involved.

The passage of the four millionth man through Calais on 15th February, 1946 (Private Neale) was the occasion of an Army Publicity exercise. His journey from his unit in Germany to the demobilization centre in the U.K. is fully recorded in photos in the Imperial War Museum. One in this book shows him being greeted by Captain T.C. Woods, the Master of the *Lady of Mann*, when he embarked on that ship.

Lt. Col. Michael Roberts, the Green Howards, succeeded Lt. Col. George Wharton as Port Commandant in March, 1946. The flow during the remainder of 1946 gradually shifted away from Germany, as Cuxhaven took over the embarkation of troops for demobilization, to Italy and Austria. Overall control of the Port was transferred from HQ BAOR to British Army Staff, France in Paris. With the run down in numbers Lt. Col. Roberts was in turn succeeded by the last Port Commandant, Major Eddison of The Manchester Regiment. I am indebted to Major Philip Kenyon for details of the final events. The Movement detachments of one Lieutenant and five men moved into No.5 Transit Camp. A priority at that time was the repatriation of those Polish troops who wished to return to their country whilst others from Italy settled in the U.K. and North America.

When sailings were reduced to one per day, the time had come for the formal military closure of the Port in the summer of 1947. After this such troop movements as did occur were made on the two civilian services i.e. the 'Golden Arrow' ship from Dover and the other route from Folkestone. For a long time the Army had a daily reservation of one 1st and one 2nd class compartment on the Calais/Paris 'Flèche d'Or'. This was a far cry from the days when three troopships, the train ferry and the mail coaster were all berthed at the same time.

PART II

Chapter 4
The Ships

The ships form the main part of this story. Before considering them in detail there are a few general points to make. Fifteen passenger ships served as troopships at various times. They were drawn from five British companies and the Belgian Marine, all French ships having been lost; such a variety is probably unique in the history of Calais. In addition there were the three Dover – Dunkirk train ferries and the Southern Railway cargo ships which acted as mail coasters. It will not surprise followers of the cross channel scene to learn that nine of the fifteen passenger ships were built by Dennys of Dumbarton.

Because obstructions were still being cleared, sailings were initially tidal but by 1st March, 1945 it was possible to operate a regular schedule. Additionally, because of the damaged state of the port, the troopships operated officially in daylight, although it was often dusk when the last ship arrived. The first ship to dock in Calais after dark was the *Canterbury* when she inaugurated the Folkestone – Calais civilian service on 1st December, 1946.

The schedule I have quoted in Chapter 3 for 2nd January, 1946 was exceptional. Particularly in the early period there was a shortage of ships because there had been inadequate time for maintenance of engines since the start of the Normandy invasion in June, 1944. This applied especially to the Belgian ships which had been on numerous Commando operations. At one stage in April, 1945 the War Diary records that only seven of the thirteen ships in the pool (see next paragraph) were serviceable.,

The ships which served Calais came under the South East Coast Ports pool of the Ministry of War Transport i.e. they also operated from Dover and Tilbury to Ostend. The crossing particularly from Tilbury was of course longer and for the most part was covered by Irish Sea ships — *Ulster Monarch, Duke of Argyll* (Hospital), *Duke of Lancaster, Duke of Rothesay,* H.M.S. *Duke of Wellington (Duke of York)* and *Longford*. Other names which appear are the Harwich – Hook ships *Vienna* and *Mecklenburg* (Dutch), the Great

Western Railway's *St Helier* and the Isle of Man Steam Packet Co.'s *Viking*.

Other ships were needed for Newhaven – Dieppe and from July, 1945 Harwich – Hook of Holland. The civilian, and, in the case of Ulster, military, claims of the Irish Sea services also had to be considered especially once the war ended.

To introduce the ships at Calais in chronological order would be tedious. The chapters which follow are therefore divided by companies and subdivided by ships. All the ships were manned by company crews under special articles (T.124) i.e. they were requisitioned by the Ministry of War Transport but flew the Red Ensign.

The exceptions were the Belgians which initially ran on Harwich – Calais as H.M.S. *Princess Astrid* and H.M.S. *Princess Josephine Charlotte*. The spelling of 'Princess' had reverted to the Flemish 'Prinses' when the *Astrid* reappeared in 1946 manned by the Belgians.

All ships carried an O.C. Troops (usually an Army Captain), a sergeant and three soldiers. They supervised, once the troops were at the ship's end of the gangway, the embarkation and disembarkation of personnel and their allocation to different decks. This was especially important to ensure a quick turnround. No meals were served on the Dover/Folkestone – Calais run though emergency rations were kept and were utilized when two incoming ships were fogbound off Calais all night.

No specific naval escorts were provided in the four months until the war ended but a duty destroyer and other craft covered the Straits generally. The crews of the ships had to keep a sharp lookout for mines which were the main danger particularly after the war. E-boat activity off Ostend posed greater problems while the war lasted. Some Landing Ships Tank and cargo ships were lost off the latter port.

Canterbury in Southampton Water prior to D. Day 1944, as Landing Ship Infantry (minus landing craft). (Henry Maxwell)

Canterbury arriving at Folkestone from Calais to open the leave service on 1st January 1945.
(Henry Maxwell/Captain Walker)

Chapter 5
Southern Railway Passenger Ships

Canterbury

It was fitting that the leave service, which saw the re-opening of Calais as a personnel port on 1st January, 1945, was entrusted to the *Canterbury*. The pre-war flagship of the Dover/Folkestone fleet had operated the legendary 'Golden Arrow' service from 1929 to the outbreak of war.

The ship had previously crossed for berthing trials on 23rd December, 1944 commanded by Captain G.D. ('Tony') Walker, D.S.C. Of this voyage Captain Walker says 'It was blowing a bit North Easterly and the port didn't look very inviting.' He was, however, congratulated on 'steaming into port like a destroyer'.

On her first trooping voyage her appearance was markedly different from her peacetime rig. Painted grey overall and with one mast, she still retained her anti-aircraft guns. Although the landing craft and their hoists had been removed, her superstructure i.e. forward boat deck and promenade (awning) deck were completely plated in. Her official wartime code name number was 'PH65' but the letters CY were painted under the bridge. She crossed from Folkestone to Calais in the morning 'in rather dirty weather', Captain Walker recalls; and returned at dusk (see photo). Although it was a grey day, the return crossing was smooth. An Army band played at Calais and the troops were welcomed to Folkestone by Lt. Col. Cedric Aldworth M.C. (Port Commandant Dover/Folkestone) with the words 'A Happy New Year. We are very pleased to see you and we hope this will be the best leave you have ever had.' The same troops returned on the *Canterbury* when she left Folkestone in the early dawn of 10th January with snow falling.

We must now go back in time for a brief history of the ship. The *Canterbury* was built by Dennys of Dumbarton in 1928/29, as a luxury ship for 300 passengers, to serve as the sea link between Dover and Calais for the famous 'Golden Arrow' all Pullman train which ran from London to Dover while the equally plush 'Flèche d'Or' ran from Calais to Paris.

Canterbury in January 1946, alongside at Calais in her last month as troopship. *Ben-My-Chree* in background.

Canterbury in June 1946, at full speed in mid-channel after re-opening the Golden Arrow Service.

Among her luxurious appointments, initially, was a Palm Court Lounge. She made her first crossing on 15th May, 1929. By the winter of 1931/32, however, the depression had caught up with the service and she was converted to carry a total of 1,400 1st and 2nd class passengers, though the Golden Arrow passengers still had the exclusive use of the boat deck lounge and the forward part of the promenade (awning) deck. The Palm Court was removed at this time.

She was requisitioned on the outbreak of war, serving initially from Southampton to Cherbourg and then as a leave ship between Dover and Boulogne. From 10th May, 1940 all was changed. 12th May found her disembarking Guardsmen at the Hook of Holland and two days later she was back off the Hook, though her Guardsmen had already been evacuated by warships. On 21st May she evacuated troops from Boulogne and on 22nd May crossed to Calais with the Queen Victoria's Rifles. The *Canterbury* is incorrectly described on pages 60 – 62 of 'The Flames of Calais' by the late Airey Neave as the 'City of Canterbury'. By a strange coincidence the Ellerman cargo liner of that name did indeed follow the *Canterbury* into Calais with vehicles and equipment as described later in this book. The story of Dunkirk has been told in detail elsewhere. Suffice it to say that the *Canterbury* made five crossings, sustained damage from bombs, which involved docking in Dover for three days, and is estimated to have evacuated some 6,500 troops. The bombing occurred on her fourth voyage on 29th May and it is a tribute to all concerned that she was back in Dunkirk on 3rd June. Captain Charles A. Hancock, who had been her regular Master since 1932, was awarded the D.S.C.

From 6th – 16th June she made various voyages from Southampton to Le Havre, Cherbourg and Brest. After a final return to Plymouth she had a well earned rest in the River Dart. 1941 and early 1942 found her operating as a troopship between Stranraer and Larne. She also served as a target ship for the Fleet Air Arm/R.A.F. After this she went to Ardrossan for an eight month conversion to a Landing Ship Infantry (Hand Hoisting). At this point Captain Hancock handed over to Captain Walker.

In the summer of 1943 she became part of 'Force J'. Naval personnel were added to her Southern Railway crew to man and maintain her six LCAs (Landing Craft Assault). On 4th June, 1944 she embarked 420 troops of the 3rd Canadian Division at Southampton and her landing craft duly landed them in two waves, the first at H. hour on D. Day in 'JUNO' sector near Courseuilles. On D + 3 she sailed from Weymouth with 800 U.S. troops for the beachhead; but her main U.K. base after that was Newhaven or, occasionally, Southampton. With the completion of the Mulberry at Arromanches, she was able to berth alongside. Following the liberation of Dieppe in September, she was soon able to use that port; and, after a much needed boiler refit, in conjunction with *Princess Maud* opened the duty service to Ostend from Dover on 7th December.

It is time to return to the events recorded in paragraphs 1 and 2. Calais was to be the *Canterbury*'s port of arrival on the far shore for the next thirteen months and Folkestone her port of departure although, after the war finished, she frequently lay in Calais overnight. Her normal complement of troops was 1,500 but at least once she embarked over 1,800. On 12th May, 1945 she departed to Southampton for a much needed refit, especially to her engines. She did not return until July but externally she looked a different ship (see photo), having been painted in Southern Railway colours. She still had only one mast, however, and her superstructure was still plated in. About this time I discovered that she had retained at least one of her partitioned staterooms (P & S) on the boat deck at the top of the main staircase. This was officially the Captain's day cabin, but was frequently given up to guests. Captain Walker's main cabin was on the bridge deck behind the wheelhouse and chartroom.

The *Canterbury* played an important part in the great gale of October, 1945. The wind increased during the day on 23rd October so that, when sailings were cancelled at noon, there were three ships in Calais and one in Dover. In addition to troops waiting for normal leave, we had 2,000 priority personnel from the Royal Pioneer Corps hastily summoned from the British Army of the Rhine by the Attlee government to assist because of a strike in the London docks. To correct the imbalance Captain Walker volunteered to sail light on 24th October when the wind was Force 10. When the gale blew itself out on 27th October, the *Canterbury* was the first ship out of Folkestone, though the condition of the paint on her bows showed a slight sign of her crossing three days earlier, and first out of Calais on 28th October. The ship was not so fortunate on 31st December, 1945, as fog descended at midday and Captain Walker and Lt. Col. Wharton, who had hoped to spend New Year's Eve together with their wives in Folkestone, were forced to remain in Calais.

Captain G.D. ('Tony') Walker, D.S.C., Master of the *Canterbury* 1943 – 52, on the spray-spattered bridge of the *Lord Warden*, his last command. (Sir Peter Allen)

Eventually in the first week of February, 1946, the *Canterbury* left for the Tyne to be refitted for the 'Golden Arrow' service. It is fitting at this stage to pay an Army tribute to Captain G.D. ('Tony') Walker, D.S.C., happily still with us at the age of 94. Captain Walker, the son and grandson of Trinity House pilots, had served initially with the Prince Line and had taken his Master's certificate at 22 during the First War when he served as Second and then Chief Officer in H.M. Transport *Italian Prince* engaged in trooping from Southampton. He joined the then South Eastern and Chatham Railway in 1919 and became a passenger ship Master of the Southern

Railway Ships in 1935. He was awarded the D.S.C. for outstanding service at Dunkirk in command of the *Maid of Orleans*. Forceful, determined but courteous, he aroused the Army's admiration not only for his ship handling ability, but also for his unfailing hospitality, which led some senior officers to telephone ahead to ask which sailing the *Canterbury* was taking so that they could travel with him. With Captain Walker on the bridge, the *Canterbury* always seemed to glide up to her berth stern first faster than any other ship. The speed of her departure meant that she had cleared the breakwater in a few minutes. On one occasion Colonel Ronnie McAlister, the Garrison Commander, who was on board to see off a departing friend, made an unexpected day trip to the U.K. as he did not realize the ship had sailed. Captain Walker would also react quickly to an emergency. When Colonel 'Jock' Ralston of 36 Beach Brick sailed in March, 1945 on posting to the Far East, he was last seen on the flying bridge of the *Canterbury* waving farewell to his friends on the quay at Calais. It was Captain Walker who restrained him from leaning too far over the rail otherwise he might have arrived back in Calais or in the water.

It was a proud day for him when Captain Walker brought the *Canterbury* back into Calais for the first Golden Arrow service for over 6½ years on 15th April, 1946. I was privileged to go on board a week later when passing through Calais, having left on posting to Rhine Army HQ in March. The transformation was incredible and Captain Walker was rightly pleased that, thanks to his insistence, the main mast had been restored.

The rest of the *Canterbury*'s tale must be briefly told. The *Invicta* replaced her as the regular Golden Arrow Ship in October, 1946 and in December she opened the Folkestone/Calais service, though from 1949 onwards her main route in the summer was to be Folkestone – Boulogne. Others may say that the *Maid of Orleans (II)*, built in 1949, was the main relief ship in winter for the *Invicta*. I only know that, when I travelled by the Golden Arrow in November, 1950, twice in November, 1956 and in December, 1960, each time it was the *Canterbury*. Captain Walker left her finally in 1952 to take command of Dover's first purpose built drive-on car ferry, the *Lord Warden*. He retired in 1958 having been Senior Master since 1955.

The *Canterbury* sailed on until 27th September, 1964 and was broken up in July, 1965 at Antwerp.

Chapter 6
Biarritz

Although the *Canterbury* takes pride of place as the first leave ship, the *Biarritz* probably carried the largest number of troops and made the most crossings through sheer length of service since she was trooping to Calais from January, 1945 until July, 1947. Apart from the *Manxman* she was the last ship on the route.

The *Biarritz* had the unique distinction of spending 15 out of her life of 34 years in government service. As it is popular nowadays to talk of the 'Blue Riband' between Dover and Calais, it is worth recording that she crossed from Dover in 57 minutes, when thirty years old, in July, 1945. She was completed by Dennys in 1915 for the South Eastern and Chatham Railway. She and her sister the *Maid of Orleans*, built three years later, were to be the last conventional two funnelled ships to appear in the Straits; not counting the twin (side by side) funnels of some of the train and car ferries. They were also the fastest British built passenger ships out of Dover or Folkestone. The *Biarritz* had classical Dennys lines. Apart from her funnels she had two tall masts; a counter stern completed a handsome profile particularly broadside on.

The ship was immediately taken up by the Admiralty on completion and used as a minelayer in the Mediterranean initially. She did not return to her owners until 1921. By this time she proudly bore a plaque reading *Breslau* 20th January, 1918. Her minelaying in the Aegean Sea had caused the sinking of that German cruiser and damage to the battle cruiser *Goeben*.

In civilian service she ran from Dover to Calais until 1925 but, with the arrival of the *Isle of Thanet* and *Maid of Kent* in that year, her primary route until 1939 was to be Folkestone – Boulogne. She was converted to burn oil fuel in the winter of 1925/6. At the same time her promenade deck was fully plated in and her funnels heightened.

On the outbreak of war, with the bulk of the Southern Railway Fleet, she was requisitioned for trooping and served as a leave ship between Dover and Boulogne from December 1939 to April 1940. She appeared briefly in Rotterdam in April, 1940, under the command of Captain Walker, when she evacuated British civilians. At the start of the German invasion of the Low Countries she was in

Biarritz arriving at Folkestone before the war. (National Railway Museum)

Biarritz leaving Calais in a strong westerly wind in July 1945. N.B. Temporary repairs to Quai, *Lady of Mann* in background.

dock at Dover, having degaussing equipment fitted against mines. She took men of the 2nd Guards Brigade from Dover to Boulogne on 22nd May.

She made a brief but tragic voyage to Dunkirk on 27th May under the command of Captain W.H. Baker. Whilst passing Gravelines she was shelled by German batteries and hit several times in the forward boiler room. Fireman A. Phillips, though severely wounded in the thigh, attempted to turn off the oil supply before reporting to Captain Baker. He died that night and was posthumously mentioned in despatches. The Chief Engineer, Mr J.L. Crockart, who was subsequently awarded the D.S.C., managed to maintain power to the three after boilers and the ship limped back to Dover and subsequently left for repairs in Southampton. However, she was back in service on the night of 19th/20th June when she evacuated the last 1,000 British troops from Guernsey together with 85 French Naval ratings and 91 civilians.

Like many other ships after the hectic summer of 1940, the next 2½ years were to be spent either trooping from Stranraer to Larne or serving the Royal Navy. The high speed of the cross channel ships made them particularly suitable for towing targets. Some of them were also involved in experimental radar work.

In 1943 the *Biarritz* was converted to a Landing Ship Infantry (Hand Hoisting) in preparation for the Normandy invasion. Although she appears to have been a reserve ship off the beaches on D-Day, she was back in Newhaven on D + 2 and sailed for the British/ Canadian sector with 800 troops. After that she ran regularly to Arromanches and later Dieppe usually from Newhaven.

The *Biarritz* (Code No.PH64) made her first appearance in Calais, since 1940, in January, 1945 on the Harwich run. She was the last ship to sail from Harwich on 27th February, 1945 when this route was closed. Externally she presented quite a dashing appearance as her camouflage was striped grey and blue rather than the uniform grey. Internally her lack of deck space made conditions rather cramped when she carried her full complement of 1,500 (500 on the Harwich route). Remarkably she still retained her handsome main staircase with some pre-war cabins on 'C' deck. These were useful if a General was embarked as the Captain's cabin on the boat deck under the bridge was small.

When she returned from her first post-war refit, her funnels were again painted in Southern Railway buff with black tops but her

Biarritz sailing from Calais as troopship in July 1945.

Biarritz leaving Calais as one of the last troopships in 1947.   (National Railway Museum)

superstructure remained grey. This made rather an unhappy compromise though she always looked a trim ship.

The *Biarritz* served almost continuously from either Dover or Folkestone to Calais from March until 8th December, 1945, when she was off for three weeks refit. She was in the Wellington Dock in Dover again in March, 1946 when a fire broke out among some lifebelts. Fortunately damage was slight.

As the traffic diminished, the larger and newer ships were gradually released but the *Biarritz* sailed steadily on until the end of 1946 when she went to the Clyde for a two months refit. She was back again on 22nd February, 1947 and maintained the now greatly reduced service until 7th July, 1947. She made a special sailing from Calais to Folkestone on 24th July, 1946 carrying an unusual complement consisting of the Italian wives of Polish servicemen who were already in the U.K.

In her initial period on the run the *Biarritz* was commanded by Captain A.E. Larkins, then by Captain S. Kingsland, later to become Mayor of Dover. Her regular Master from October, 1945 was Captain Cecil Masters. Captain Masters had commanded the Southern Railway's small car ferry *Autocarrier* at Dunkirk and subsequently switched to the Train Ferries. He was a 'gentle' man in the best sense of the word; very quietly spoken, it was reputed that he only had to whisper his orders for the crew to respond. He must, I think, have been saddened by the loss of the *Maid of Orleans* (younger sister of the *Biarritz*) which was mined and sunk off Normandy on the night of 28th June, 1944 when returning light from the beaches. Captain Masters was serving as Relief Master, and although apparently imperturbable at the time — he returned to the ship for his Rolls Razor and best cap — this must have left its mark particularly as four members of the engine room crew were killed. But his courtesy never failed. Returning with him from Dover on Easter Monday, 1946 at about 1600 hrs his steward produced a tray with biscuits and a silver tea pot which was a fairly unusual sight in a Master's cabin at that time. He remained the ship's regular Master until 1947 but his health deteriorated and he died in April, 1949 at the early age of 49.

The end of the *Biarritz* can also be swiftly told. From the summer of 1947 she was based on Harwich for a year ferrying not troops but displaced persons and other unusual personnel to the Hook of Holland, though she reappeared in Dover for overhaul in November, 1947. Eventually released in Southampton, to what was by then the

39

British Transport Commission, in August, 1948, her accommodation and more particularly her engines were too run down to be worthy of repair. Finally and fittingly she was towed back to Dover in November, 1949. My last sight of her was lying in the Wellington Dock at Christmas that year. By then she looked even more incongruous as the bridge was painted white while the superstructure remained grey. Subsequently she was broken up on the beach inside the Eastern Arm. Her War Service plaque is in the Castle Cornet Maritime Museum, Guernsey.

Chapter 7
Invicta

There was great excitement in Calais on Boxing Day, 1945, when 5½ years after her completion, the *Invicta* (Code No.PH67) sailed into the port, for the first time. She presented a completely different profile from any previous Southern Railway ship. Whereas the *Canterbury*, although with some unique features, had been in many ways a development of the *Isle of Thanet* and *Maid of Kent* (sunk at Dieppe as a hospital ship in May, 1940), the *Invicta*, with four enclosed decks and built up forward, was 1,000 tons larger than the *Canterbury*. She had a huge funnel, wide rather than tall, and looked her best broadside on. Unlike the three previous ships she had no covered passenger accommodation on the boat deck, the whole forward structure under the bridge being devoted to officers' cabins so that, when Lt. Col. George Wharton and I went to call on Captain Payne on that first morning of 26th December, 1945, we were confronted by a whole corridor of cabins.

Laid down by Dennys in 1939 to replace the *Canterbury* on the 'Golden Arrow' route, her engines were initially fitted to burn Kent coal. She was converted to oil in 1946 and was the first Dover ship to be fitted with stabilizers in 1949.

Completed in 1940, she was laid up in the Clyde but eventually was commissioned by the Royal Navy as a Fleet transport under the White Ensign. It was not in fact until April, 1942 that the Chief of Combined Operations called for additional ships. The *Invicta* was among those selected. She was converted to a Landing Ship Infantry (Hand Hoisting) by Barclay Curle at Elderslie on the Clyde and was commissioned on 3rd June, 1942 under the command of Commander T.L. Owen, R.N.R. Her 'upper deck', i.e. officers and seamen, were drawn from the Royal Navy but the engine room staff and stewards came from the Merchant Navy under T124X (special articles). She was ready for service on 14th June only two months after conversion had begun. The work had involved some cutting away of the boat deck superstructure and the six LCAs (Landing Craft Assault) were slung outboard, unlike lifeboats.

After various rehearsals and a postponement, her first assignment was on the ill-fated expedition to Dieppe on 19th August, 1942. She

Invicta being fitted out as Landing Ship Infantry on the Clyde in May 1942.

(Imperial War Museum)

Invicta arriving as troopship at Dover from Calais on 15th April 1946. N.B. Foremast of *Canterbury* in background dressed overall to mark re-opening of Golden Arrow service after nearly 7 years.

embarked the South Saskatchewan Regiment at Southampton under the command of Lieutenant Colonel Cecil Merritt who gained the V.C. The voyage over was marred by a grenade explosion, which wounded seventeen soldiers. Although she lay off Dieppe for nine hours, the ship herself was not damaged. Her permanent crew at this time consisted of 14 officers and 41 ratings and 6 other R.N. officers and 67 ratings to man the landing craft and the anti-aircraft defences.

The *Invicta* came under command of Force 'J' in October, 1943 in preparation for Normandy. She was still under the White Ensign as were H.M.S *Duke of Wellington* (the London, Midland and Scottish Railway's Heysham ship *Duke of York*) and H.M.S. *Brigadier* (the Southern Railway's Newhaven ship *Worthing*). For the initial assault she embarked 450 troops at Southampton and these were landed in two waves. She sailed again on D + 4 for the U.S. sector.

For the next four months her work was similar to that of the *Canterbury* but, with the opening of Ostend in December, 1944, her U.K. home port became Tilbury. She carried duty personnel to and from the Belgian port until April. She was then detailed for Operation 'Nestegg', the liberation of the Channel Islands, and carried relief forces to Jersey on 8th May, remaining in the area until her return to Tilbury on 22nd May. The troops were landed in Jersey from LCAs.

She was finally paid off by the Royal Navy on 9th October, 1945 and was refitted in the London docks. She appeared in Dover for the first time on 21st December, 1945, again, like the *Canterbury*, in Southern Railway colours but with only one mast and her promenade deck still plated in.

She served as a troopship on the Dover – Calais route for only four months from 26th December, 1945 until 22nd April, 1946. Her additional enclosed deck space meant that she normally carried 1,750 troops, though, on one occasion, when she was the last ship of the day out of Dover and they had a backlog to clear, she arrived in Calais with 2,200 on board. Her extra space below decks meant less discomfort particularly in rough weather. Two mishaps, one minor, one tragic, marked her stay on the route. On 27th December, 1945 she collided with the *Ben-My-Chree* in Dover due to a bridge telegraph defect. On 24th January, 1946 her 4th Engineer was crushed by a watertight door and sadly killed.

She left for the Tyne on 23rd April, 1946 to be fitted out to succeed the *Canterbury* on the 'Golden Arrow' service. I have speculated that the four months trooping was to enable the ship and her officers and

Invicta alongside at Calais in 1947 on 'Golden Arrow' service. N.B. Southern Railway flag at main mast. (National Railway Museum)

crew to accustom themselves to Calais. But on this point Captain Walker, who periodically relieved Captain Payne, comments that her additional deck forward was well compensated for by the extra engine power and she handled beautifully. Captain John Arthur (see Chaper 17) confirms this.

The main reason was that both the British and French Governments, despite the shortages, were anxious to restore the 'Golden Arrow' service as quickly as possible as a morale boosting measure, particularly as the only route to France for civilians after the war was Newhaven – Dieppe. The *Canterbury* took only three months to be restored to her pre-war glory. The *Invicta*, which had never been fitted out as a peacetime ship and had to be converted to oil fuel, took six months.

Both during her service as a troopship at Calais, and, until his death in 1955, the *Invicta* had only one regular Master, Captain L.H. ('Len') Payne O.B.E., Légion d'Honneur. Born in 1892, he joined the South Eastern and Chatham Railway in 1920. He was the first Captain of the Train Ferries to Dunkirk and served as Master of the

Hampton Ferry when she operated early in the war as the minelayer H.M.S. *Hampton*. During this time he held a R.N.R. commission as a Lieutenant Commander, which enabled him to fly the Blue Ensign in peacetime on the *Invicta*. From 1942-1944 he commanded the *Maid of Orleans* though he was not in command when she was lost (see *Biarritz*). He succeeded Captain Hancock as Commodore of the Southern Railway Fleet in 1947.

He was an outsize character in every sense of the word. Although his favourite adjective was 'bleeding', he was a kindly bluff God-fearing man. His words to his crew of the *Maid of Orleans* before Normandy are worth recording: 'I am no hero and would rather be working in my garden. But there is a job to be done for our country and I know that you will do it'. He also reminded them that, like the *Maid* after whom the ship was named, they too were going to liberate France. He died suddenly in his cabin on the *Invicta*, fifteen minutes before the ship was due to sail on 19th December, 1955.

The *Invicta* herself took over the 'Golden Arrow' service from the *Canterbury* on 15th October, 1946. She remained on this route until 8th August, 1972 when she was superceded by the car ferry *Horsa*. After a six weeks lay up at Newhaven she was towed away to be broken up in the Netherlands on 21st September, 1972. No country by then had any use for a 32-year-old ship which did not carry cars.

Dinard as Hospital Ship off the Isle of Wight.   (Imperial War Museum)

Dinard arriving at Dover from Calais as troopship in August 1946.

Chapter 8
Other Southern Railway Ships

A *Dinard*

The *Dinard* served as a troopship between Dover and Calais for a period of three months from June to August, 1946.

She was built by Dennys in 1924 with her sister *St Briac*, which was mined and sunk in the North Sea in 1942, for the Southampton – St Malo service. They were the first ships to be ordered by the Southern Railway, after its formation in 1923, and the first to be built to burn oil fuel. With a gross tonnage of 2,291 tons they were also the largest units in the Southampton based fleet at that time.

The *Dinard* remained on the St Malo route until the war. On 2nd October, 1939 she was requisitioned as a hospital ship based on Newhaven. This port was registered under the Geneva Convention as the main U.K. base for all cross channel hospital carriers. The *Dinard* made three voyages to Dunkirk and transported about 1,000 stretcher cases to Newhaven. Her last voyage, particularly, was marked by the usual hail of bombs and shells. Admittedly it was made at night but two hospital ships, the *Brighton* and *Maid of Kent* had already been sunk in daylight in Dieppe. Among the three members of *Dinard*'s crew Mentioned in Despatches was Mrs Goodrich, a stewardess in peace time. She was the only woman to receive an award at Dunkirk. The *Dinard*'s Chief Officer and acting Master, Captain J. Ailwyn Jones, was also Mentioned in Despatches as was Mr Norman Smith, Chief Engineer.

After Dunkirk the *Dinard* served at Scapa Flow. July, 1943, however, found her operating off Sicily as a hospital carrier and later that year in the Italian invasions. Except for the *Brittany* which served with the Eastern Fleet, the *Dinard* was the only Southern Railway ship to sail so far afield.

By the spring of 1944 she was back in the Channel in preparation for Normandy but her first voyage to the beaches on 7th June, 1944 nearly ended in disaster. She struck a mine on her way to the Juno Sector and was eventually towed back to Southampton 'with her forepart nearly falling off'. Permanent repairs took a considerable time but, surprisingly, she appeared in Dover in February, 1945 with the Great Western Railway's *St Julien*, both as hospital carriers,

Dinard sailing from Dover to Boulogne as car ferry in 1950.   (Skyfotos)

operating to Boulogne. They were the first personnel ships to enter this port and, in view of the destruction of the Quai Gare Maritime, berthed opposite at the Quai des Excursionnistes at the seaward end of the Quai Gambetta. This quay was used before and after the war by the General Steam Navigation Co. and P & A Campbell for their day trips.

May, 1945 found the *Dinard* back at Newhaven. Her 5½ years stint as a hospital ship was now over and she assisted in trooping duties to Dieppe but more frequently from Southampton to Le Havre.

When she appeared in Calais on her first visit to the port at the beginning of June, 1946, she was in Southern Railway colours and looked similar to her peacetime appearance. Her interior had of course not been gutted as much as the troopships which made for more comfortable conditions although her deck space with 1,500 on board was limited.

The *Dinard*'s Masters during her Calais service are listed as Captain W.A. Harper, who came with her from Newhaven, and Captain R.E. Gartside, formerly Chief Officer of the *Canterbury*.

In the autumn of 1946 the *Dinard* was handed back to the Southern Railway and set a precedent as the first cross channel 'classic'

48

passcngcr ship to bc convertcd into a car ferry. At Palmers Yard at Hebburn-on-Tyne, she was almost completely rebuilt. To begin with her hull had been slightly hogged and twisted by the mine off Normandy and this required attention. In addition her main deck was completely stripped for the carriage of cars, an opening was cut in the promenade deck at the stern to permit loading and all her accommodation on the promenade and boat decks was altered. New masts and funnels and bridge structure completed the transformation. In June, 1947 she returned to Dover with accommodation for 361 passengers and 70 cars. Until 1952 the cars had to be lifted on, but with the completion of ramps at Dover and Boulogne, stern doors were inserted at the after end of the main deck to enable cars to be driven on over the stern.

The arrival of the new *Maid of Kent* in 1959 made her redundant and she was sold to Rederi A/B Vikinlinjen, Finland. She ran for another eleven years as a car ferry in the Baltic with only minor modifications. She was renamed *Viking* and thus became the first of the many ships of that name, one of which now runs on the Sally Line service from Ramsgate to Dunkirk. Having been resold in 1965 to Rederi A/B Solstad, Finland, she remained in service until 1970 and was not finally scrapped until 1974 in her fiftieth year.

B *Isle of Guernsey*

The *Isle of Guernsey* ran from Calais to Newhaven in conjunction with the *Victoria* from 1st – 20th April, 1945. This was a temporary service while the second berth at Folkestone was being dredged for permanent use. The ships carried only 750 troops because of the longer crossing. This was the only time *Isle of Guernsey* ever served Calais.

The *Isle of Guernsey* was built by Dennys in 1930 for the Southampton – Channel Islands route as one of a trio of ships, the others being *Isle of Jersey* (1930) and *Isle of Sark* (1932). The gross tonnage of the *Isle of Guernsey* was 2,180 gross tons and she was powered by four Parsons turbines giving a service speed of 19 knots.

On the outbreak of war she was converted to a hospital ship (Hospital Carrier No.26) based on Newhaven and, as such, made at least three crossings to Dunkirk. On 26th May she evacuated 346 stretcher cases. On 29th May, despite her Red Cross markings she suffered damage from bombs, cannon fire from aircraft and shelling. It was

Isle of Guernsey as a troopship off South Coast in December 1944. *Biarritz* had similar camouflage until May 1945. (John de S. Winter)

on this voyage that Able Seaman Fowles went down a rope ladder to try and rescue a British pilot in the sea. He was wounded and swept away but was fortunately rescued by another ship. *Isle of Guernsey* was back at Dunkirk on 30th May and evacuated another 400 wounded. By then, however, the cumulative damage was so severe that she was unable to make any more crossings. The ship's Master, Captain E.L. Hill was awarded the D.S.C., as was the Chief Engineer, Mr D. Robb. A.B. John Fowles received the D.S.M., and Mr R.F. Pembury, the Chief Officer, was Mentioned in Despatches. This was the largest number of awards to be received by any hospital ship.

Isle of Guernsey was fitted out at Cardiff in the autumn of 1940 for service in the Firth of Clyde area as a Fleet Air Arm/R.A.F. target ship. In early 1943 she became a radar training ship but, between September, 1943 and January, 1944 she was converted to a Landing Ship Infantry (Hand Hoisting) in preparation for Normandy. As part of Force 'J2' she sailed from Southampton and landed Canadian troops at Bernieres in Juno Sector on D-Day. She was the second vessel to enter the Mulberry harbour at Arromanches when that remarkable feat of engineering was able to receive troopships at the end of June, 1944.

After that, except for two diversions, Newhaven was to be her main U.K. base for over two years. Having been stripped of her

Landing Craft, in mid January, 1945 whilst the war was still in progress, she restored the first civilian service to France (Dieppe) on a tri-weekly basis for priority passengers and military personnel.

As the excellent photo shows, she still looked very much a military ship during her three week stint on the Calais route, with her prominent dazzle camouflage of blue, grey and black and a number of anti-aircraft guns. The camouflage was similar to that of the *Biarritz* but no picture of the latter ship painted thus remains. It is an interesting question why some ships retained this camouflage, whilst others e.g. the *Canterbury, Lady of Mann* and *Ben-My-Chree* were grey overall. Perhaps the simple answer was availability of paint.

Isle of Guernsey's second and more appropriate diversion from Newhaven was to reopen the passenger service from Southampton to Guernsey and Jersey on 25th June, 1945. But she only stayed on the route for ten days being relieved by *Hantonia* on 6th July.

After this it was back to Newhaven – Dieppe. The ship was aground in Dieppe Harbour for nine hours on 30th October, 1945 suffering some damage. She finally left the route in late 1946 but conversion took some months due to hull damage resulting from her grounding in Dieppe. The French built *Londres*, which the Germans had used during the war, was able to join *Worthing* on the regular run from Newhaven – Dieppe in April, 1947.

From April 1947 until 1960, *Isle of Guernsey* ran regularly to the Channel Islands. In the winter of 1960 she operated a much reduced service, her two sisters having already gone with the arrival of the new *Caesarea* in 1960 to be followed by *Sarnia* in 1961. *Isle of Guernsey* made her last sailing from Southampton on 12th May, 1961 then moved to Weymouth briefly making her final crossing from there on 16th June. She was finally broken up at Ghent in November, 1961.

Of the pre-war Southern Railway Dover/Folkestone fleet, the *Maid of Kent* and *Maid of Orleans*, as already recorded, were lost during the war. The only ship which did not visit Calais as a troopship was the *Isle of Thanet*. After serving as flagship of Force 'J' at Normandy, she was required for trooping and Government service from January, 1945 until late 1946 between Newhaven and Dieppe due to the fact that all but one of the pre-war fleet on this route had been lost or rendered unserviceable. As a result she did not appear in Calais until February, 1947 when she relieved the *Canterbury* on the civilian Folkestone – Calais service.

Princess Maud at sea pre-war.   (National Maritime Museum)

Princess Maud between Stranraer and Larne in 1942.   (National Maritime Museum)

Chapter 9
London, Midland and Scottish Railway

Princess Maud (Code No.PH76)

The *Princess Maud* of the London, Midland and Scottish Railway was the only other railway owned ship to run to Calais. Her home port was Stranraer but during her service in the Straits of Dover in 1939 – 40 and 1944 – 45 she achieved a number of distinctions. She was one of the last three ships out of Dunkirk in 1940 and was off the Normandy beaches on D-Day 6th June, 1944. With the *Canterbury* she reopened Ostend to personnel ships on 7th December, 1944 and on 4th January, 1945 was the second personnel ship to enter Calais.

The *Princess Maud* was launched by Lady Craigavon, wife of the Prime Minister of Northern Ireland, on 19th December, 1933. Built by Dennys at a cost of only £160,000 she was, at 2,886 gross tons, a slightly larger version of the *Princess Margaret* built in 1931. The name Maud may sound unfashionable now but she replaced an earlier ship of the same name (1904 – 31). She was in fact named after King George Vth's sister, who was Queen of Norway until her death in 1938 and mother of the present King Olav.

The ship was certified to carry 1,458 passengers with sleeping accommodation for 233 (161 1st Class and 62 3rd Class) and had 43,000 cubic feet of cargo space. The 'cargo' might include cars or cattle. With an observation lounge under the bridge and a smoking room further aft on the boat deck plus a partly enclosed promenade deck, she and her sister provided a greatly improved service on the Stranraer – Larne route. The *Maud* made her first voyage as flagship on 1st March, 1934 and served without incident until the outbreak of war. Originally built to burn coal she was converted to oil at Dennys early in 1939. However there was something of a revolution in 1939 when the first purpose built British car ferry the *Princess Victoria* appeared. Stranraer was the first railway port to be equipped with a drive on ramp; the small tidal range (9′) made this an easier task than in the Channel. The *Princess Victoria* only ran for two months before the war, when she was requisitioned as a minelayer, but was herself sunk by a mine off the Humber on 21st May, 1940.

Princess Maud arriving at Calais as troopship in May 1945. The Clocktower of Hotel de Ville is in background.

The *Princess Maud* was requisitioned immediately on the outbreak of war and served as a troopship from Southampton or Dover. She was under repair when the Dunkirk evacuation began and therefore made only two crossings. On the first on 30th May, 1940, she was hit by shells off Gravelines, one of which punctured the engine room, wounding four of the crew who subsequently died. Captain H.L. Clarke tried to continue to Dunkirk but the inflow of water meant that she had to return to Dover and enter the Wellington Dock for repairs. However she was back on the last night of the evacuation and was alongside the breakwater under shellfire from midnight on 3rd June until 0200 hrs on 4th June when she left with a full load. The *Maud* with the Isle of Man Steam Packet Co.'s *Tynwald* and the General Steam Navigation Co.'s *Royal Sovereign* were the last personnel ships out of Dunkirk.

She was next at St Valery-en-Caux and managed to evacuate 800 troops of the 51st (Highland) Division from nearby Veules les Roses. She later evacuated troops from St Malo.

By July, 1940, however, she was back at Stranraer and remained there until November, 1943. She normally operated as a troopship but periodically relieved *Princess Margaret* on the mail run. In November, 1943 she went to Liverpool to be converted to a Landing Ship Infantry (Hand Hoisting).

After various rehearsals she sailed from Portland on 5th June as part of Force 'J2', and appeared off the Normandy beaches at Vierville early on D-Day, with 380 U.S. Army Engineers on board and 20 tons of explosives and demolition charges for demolishing beach obstacles. She sailed again from Weymouth on D + 2 and D + 4 to the U.S. sector and altogether took 16,000 troops to the beaches off Arromanches. She first arrived at Dover from Arromanches on 21st October, 1944 but was sent to Southampton for a refit and restoration of superstructure following removal of Landing Craft. After Normandy, as already recorded, she opened the Dover – Ostend duty route on 7th December, 1944 and ran on this service until the end of the month — except on the 24th when E-boats were reported off Ostend.

We first saw the *Maud* in Calais on 4th January, 1945. Except for periods in May and July, when she relieved the *Canterbury* or *Biarritz* at Folkestone, she was essentially a Dover based ship during the nine months she served Calais. Painted in grey/blue camouflage with a black top to her funnel, she retained her two masts, though the mainmast may have been replaced only after Normandy (see photo).

By chance I crossed three times on the *Maud* — once in February, 1945 and twice in July, 1945. I was struck by the fact that her accommodation had been less gutted than some of the other ships. In particular, she retained a number of cabins. These would have been useful for Generals when the 'Rhine Army Special' sleeper train, made up of stock previously used by the senior Nazi hierarchy, commenced its nightly run from Rhine Army HQ at Bad Oeynhausen to Calais and back in the evening. Unfortunately the service only started in October after the *Maud* was derequisitioned.

An indication of the ship's value may be judged from the only set of figures available for an individual vessel which show that she carried 42,074 troops from Calais to Dover in March, 1945 and 38,764 in the reverse direction. Her capacity was 1,500, and, as the personnel ships were normally based in the U.K. overnight until the end of the war and only made one crossing in each direction, the *Maud* sailed every day in that month.

The ship was involved in only one incident. On 13th May, 1945 she grounded when leaving Calais at 1815 hrs on a very low tide. The troops were disembarked and the ship refloated at 0030 hrs on the 14th. The troops were re-embarked and the ship sailed at 0630 hrs for

Folkestone. A quick inspection in dock at Dover revealed no damage and she was back in service on 16th May.

The *Maud* was an exceptionally easy ship to load and broke the record on one occasion by offloading 1,200 troops and embarking 1,500 in 35 minutes. She had almost become part of the Calais scene when it was decided in September, 1945 that she was required back at Stranraer.

This was only logical as the civilian traffic requirements to Ireland and particularly to Ulster were much heavier at this stage than those to the Continent. She made her last crossing from Calais to Dover in mid September. By then she had transported 636,000 troops on the Calais route. All told she carried 1,360,870 troops during her war service. She never returned to Calais in the remaining 27½ years of her life.

The *Princess Maud*'s regular Master was Captain Samuel (Sam) Iles. He had taken command of her in 1943 and served throughout her Normandy, Ostend and Calais experiences. We remember Captain Iles as a quiet courteous man devoted to the efficient running of his ship. I am indebted to his widow for the following account of his career. Born in 1902, he began his seagoing career at Goole in Yorkshire in 1929. He had spells at Holyhead and with the Clyde Services before arriving at Stranraer in 1933. He served as a second officer on both *Princess Margaret* and *Princess Maud* and was appointed Chief Officer in 1936. In this capacity he was present during her war service in the Channel in 1939/40. Appointed Master of the *Princess Margaret* in 1941, he subsequently was given command of the *Maud* and continued as her Master throughout 1944/45. When the *Maud* was transferred to Holyhead, he reverted to the *Margaret* and remained her Master until his premature death in October, 1958 after a long illness. The 'Stranraer Gazette' records that 'he was held in high esteem by all who knew him. The travelling public liked him. His crew regarded him as their friend and he held the complete confidence of those responsible for the Service'. His Chief Officer and Relief Master at Calais was Captain John F.D. Hay.

Like another Stranraer ship in later years, the *Caledonian Princess*, the *Maud* became something of a nomad after the war. Although she initially took over her old run from 1st October, 1945 to 18th September, 1946, her main role after that was as third ship at

Holyhead but she relieved at Stranraer on fourteen occasions between 28th October, 1946 and 7th March, 1961.

During the coal crisis in early 1947 she maintained the Holyhead – Dun Laoghaire service on her own as the only oil fired ship on the route. With the arrival of the new *Cambria* and *Hibernia* in 1949, she sailed mainly in the summer acting as relief ship on Fishguard – Waterford and Heysham – Belfast as well as Stranraer – Larne during the winter. The summer of 1951 found her operating from Southampton to St Malo or the Channel Islands. One sad task which fell to her on 2nd February, 1953 was to bring home the body of Captain Fergusson and two other victims after the loss of the *Princess Victoria* on 31st January, 1953.

The arrival of the new car ferry *Holyhead Ferry I* meant the end for the *Maud*. She made her last sailing from Holyhead on 4th September, 1965 nearly a year after the last voyage of her old running mate the *Canterbury*. But, unlike the *Canterbury*, she did not go for scrap but was sold to Lefkosia Compania Naviera S.A. of Panama with her port of registry Famagusta in Cyprus. As the *Venus*, after considerable alteration, she began a weekly service of cruises in June, 1966 between Piraeus – Limassol – Haifa – Piraeus – Brindisi – Piraeus under the management of Cyprus Sea Cruises (Limassol) Limited.

This lasted for three years after which she was sold to the Danish shipbuilding firm of Burmeister and Wain, who renamed her *Nybo*, and used her as an accommodation ship at Copenhagen for shipyard workers. She called briefly at Dover in August, 1969 en route to Copenhagen. After three years she was sold for breaking up and arrived at Bilbao in tow on 13th January, 1973 where she found the remains of another Calais friend, the *Shepperton Ferry*. The *Invicta* was the last of the Calais passenger ships to remain in service but the *Dinard*, incredibly after 49 years, and the *Princess Maud* were the last actually to reach the breakers' yard. However, Calais never saw the *Maud* again after 1945 and neither did I.

Chapter 10
Isle of Man Steam Packet Co. Ltd

Next to the Southern Railway, the Isle of Man Steam Packet Company provided the most ships on the Calais route. Due to the large capacity of the *Lady of Mann* and *Ben-My-Chree* (2,200) and the fact that the *Victoria* spent 22 months on the route, they must have carried almost as many passengers as the Southern Railway ships and their service proved invaluable.

Lady of Mann (Code No.PH75)

The *Lady of Mann*, the flagship of the fleet, first appeared in Calais a few times on the Harwich route during January and February, 1945. From April, 1945 until her demobilization at the beginning of March, 1946 she was regularly based at Dover. Like the other two ships with normal capacities above 1,500 i.e. the *Ben-My-Chree* and *Invicta*, she never ran from Folkestone partly because the Admiralty Pier at Dover could handle the larger number of troops more easily, partly because there was more protection at Dover Marine Station for ships with higher freeboard. In addition their draught was greater.

The *Lady of Mann* was built by Vickers at Barrow as the Company's Centenary ship. She was launched by the Duchess of Atholl, *the* Lady of Mann, on 4th March, 1930. Although the *Ben-My-Chree* (IV) of 1927 had set a new standard of luxury, the *Lady* surpassed her, particularly her splendid mahogany main staircase. The woodwork naturally had to be removed during the war and, although restored afterwards, the fire regulations of the 1960s caused further alterations. Her gross tonnage of 3,104 was little more than e.g. the *Canterbury*, but her peacetime passenger capacity was 2,873. This was largely because she possessed four covered decks below the boat deck. At 360' she was one of the longest of the ships on the run. Her service speed was 22 knots but she could exceed 23 knots and her horsepower of 11,500 gave her a reserve of power. She was oil fired from the start. Her tall, well proportioned funnel and clean lines gave a pleasing profile in peacetime.

Lady of Mann at full speed off the Scottish coast in 1942.   (Richard Danielson)

Her first nine years in service were uneventful. But with the majority of the fleet, she was immediately requisitioned on the outbreak of war and served as a troopship between the Channel ports and France. As for so many, the testing time came at Dunkirk. Eight of the Isle of Man ships were involved and three — *King Orry* (1913), *Fenella* (1937) and *Mona's Queen* (1934) were lost. *Tynwald* (1937) was sunk off North Africa in 1942 which meant that none of the three passenger ships built after the *Lady of Mann* before the war survived. As for Dunkirk, the Company's ships are estimated to have brought back nearly 25,000 troops i.e. roughly 1 in 14 of the total evacuated.

Lady of Mann made three voyages to Dunkirk. On 31st May she berthed at 1330 hrs. Though not equipped as a hospital carrier, she embarked a heavy load of casualties. She received some damage from shelling and bombing but left for Folkestone at 5 pm. Daylight sailings were difficult after this but the night of 1st June found her again at Dunkirk from 2300 hrs until 0200 hrs on 2nd June, when she returned to Dover. She was back again on the evening of 2nd June, but could not berth initially owing to the low tide. Eventually she pulled out at 0145 hrs on the 3rd with a heavy load. All told, she brought away about 4,260 troops. Captain T.C. Woods, the Commodore of the Fleet, was Mentioned in Despatches and subsequently received the O.B.E.

Lady of Mann leaving Calais as troopship in November 1945.

After Dunkirk, she worked westward along the coast and evacuated troops in turn from Le Havre, Cherbourg and Brest. She was estimated to have 5,000 troops on board when leaving Le Havre under aerial attack.

From August, 1940 until the spring of 1944, her work differed from any so far recorded as she transported service personnel mainly from Invergordon or Aberdeen to the Shetlands and Faroes. Briefly, however, she was based in Belfast Lough acting as a tender to the *Queen Mary* to enable the latter to turn round more quickly.

April, 1944 found her being converted to a Landing Ship Infantry (Hand Hoisting). As such she carried up to 490 Canadians in the initial assault as headquarters ship of the 512th Assault Flotilla in the Juno sector. She continued her sailings to the beaches and subsequently Cherbourg. But, with the opening of Ostend in December, 1944, she became part of the South East Coast ports pool sailing from Tilbury or Dover except for the Harwich – Calais voyages already recorded. From August, 1945 she ran regularly to Calais. I can testify to this as I crossed on her four times between September, 1945 and January, 1946.

Both the *Lady* and the *Ben* like most of the ships, had only one mast and the superstructures were plated in. They could, however, be

Lady of Mann off Douglas after the war.   (Richard Danielson)

distinguished by the flying bridge above the wheelhouse of the *Lady*, whereas the *Ben*'s bridge superstructure was at the forward end of the boat deck. Both ships remained in battleship grey until they were released. Having lost their three newest ships, the Isle of Man Company were naturally pressing for the early return of one or both of their two largest ships. Moreoever, unlike the Southern Railway, they had no marine workshops available in the South. As 1945 wore on, the two ships looked rather war weary externally, but this did not affect their performance or their interior. The first ship to appear in the Isle of Man colours in Calais was the *Victoria* in April, 1946.

The *Lady*'s crossings to Calais were for the most part uneventful. On New Year's Eve, 1945 she had to lie outside Calais all night (together with *Royal Daffodil*) when fog suddenly descended on her last crossing of the day from Dover. A happier occasion occurred on 15th February, 1946 when she embarked the 4 millionth man to pass through Calais. This event is fully recorded in photographs.

Eventually the time came for the *Lady* herself to be demobilized. She returned to Douglas on 8th March, 1946 to a civic reception. After a limited reconditioning at Birkenhead, she was able to resume service in the summer of 1946 but received a more thorough conversion to her peacetime standards in the ensuing winter.

Lady of Mann leaving the Isle of Man on her last voyage on 15th August 1971.
(Maux Technical Publications)

From 1937, and throughout the war until his retirement in 1946, the *Lady* was commanded by Captain T.C. (Tom or 'Daddy') Woods, O.B.E. It is a remarkable tribute to his stamina that he was already 60 in 1940 (hence his nickname) and, as such, was the second oldest of the Captains. Born in December, 1879, he had joined the Company as long ago as 1897. On his return to Douglas he remarked that he had taken her away in 1939 and brought her back in one piece. He then went ashore to begin a well earned retirement, after nine years as Commodore. His retirement lasted 25 years until his death in October, 1971 at the age of 91.

He will be remembered as a quiet, kindly man, though he could be a stern disciplinarian. As the photograph shows, however, he usually had a twinkle in his eye.

The *Lady* sailed on in peacetime until 1971. She became increasingly expensive to run, so that, with the completion of the post-war building programme in 1955, she only appeared in summer when her deck space proved of great advantage. However, her engines remained in good condition to the last. She sailed from Liverpool for Douglas on her last crossing on 14th August, 1971 and then sailed light from Douglas to Barrow the next day for lay up. As recorded above, her Master and Commodore for so long, Captain Woods, died in October of the same year. The *Lady* left Barrow in January, 1972 to be broken up by Arnold Young and Co. in Glasgow. So ended the life of one of the most handsome and efficient ships ever to serve the Isle of Man.

Chapter 11
Ben-My-Chree ('Girl of my Heart' in Manx)
(Code No.PH81)

The *Ben-My-Chree*, fourth ship of that name, was basically an 'Ostend' ship and did not appear in Calais until the end of January, 1946 before the departure of the *Canterbury*. She then ran throughout from Dover until her release on 9th May, 1946. This meant that, during February, 1946 we had the unusual luxury of three ships with above average capacity running out of Dover. The *Ben* (2,200 troops) joined the *Lady of Mann* (2,200) and *Invicta* (1,750).

The fourth *Ben-My-Chree* was built for the Isle of Man Steam Packet Company Limited by Cammell Laird, Birkenhead in 1927. The third ship of that name, which was flagship from 1908 – 14 was the fastest vessel ever to serve the Company. She operated as a seaplane carrier in the Mediterranean in World War I and was sunk off Castellerizo, an island off the Turkish coast on 11th January, 1917. The revival of the name was therefore popular.

Like the *Lady of Mann* she was built as an oil burner and, by coincidence, her gross tonnage and passenger capacity were the same at 2,586. Her fittings and especially her main staircase built of walnut were luxurious but, due to modern fire regulations, we shall never see the like of them again. She only remained the flagship for three years as the *Lady of Mann* arrived in 1930. The *Ben* was easily distinguished from the *Lady* due to her lower bridge, the wheelhouse, chartroom, Master's cabin and bridge wing cabs all being at the forward end of the boat deck. There were also other differences but this was the most noticeable. The *Ben*'s funnel cowl, wider than the top of the funnel, was larger than that of the *Lady*. Her funnel was shortened in 1947 and the cowl removed in 1950.

After 13 years peacetime service the *Ben*, together with nine other ships of the company's fleet, was requisitioned during the first week of the war. She served in the English Channel as a troopship initially. In the grim days of May, 1940 she brought back 4,095 troops in three crossings from Dunkirk. The numbers would have been greater but shortly after leaving Folkestone on 2nd June, 1940, with a relief crew, she was in collision and took no further part in the operation.

63

Ben-My-Chree off Douglas before the war.   (Richard Danielson)

Ben-My-Chree leaving Calais as troopship in March 1946.

She was subsequently involved, however, in evacuations from Brest and La Pallice.

It is a tribute to her seakeeping qualities that she then spent 3½ years trooping from Scottish ports (Invergordon or Cromarty) to the Northern Isles particularly the Faroes and occasionally to Iceland. On one rough voyage to Iceland from Stornaway she outstripped her escorting destroyer.

January, 1944 found her at North Shields being converted to a Landing Ship Infantry (Hand Hoisting). As such she was present off Normandy on D-Day, having sailed as part of Force 'J' from Southampton with 420 Assault Troops of U.S. Rangers. On D + 2 she made her second sailing, this time from Newhaven, in company with the *Biarritz*, the two ships carrying 1,600 troops between them. After that, in common with most of the ships in this story, she worked from Southampton or Newhaven to Arromanches or Cherbourg before moving up Channel in December, 1944. Her first crossing to Ostend was from Portsmouth on 8th December when she and *Lady of Mann* joined the convoy ex Dover.

From then until January, 1946 her U.K. base was to be Tilbury or Dover and her port of destination on the far shore, Ostend. She was among the early ships to use Dover, her first sailing from there being on 23rd December, 1944. On 2nd January, 1945 she was in collision in the Yantlet channel with the cargo ship *Fort St Paul*. Although she made port under her own steam, she was under repair for a month. The *Ben*'s picture appeared in all the national newspapers on 19th June, 1945, when she arrived at Dover from Ostend with the first draft of troops to be demobilized from the British Army of the Rhine.

Her service on the Dover – Calais route produced no major incidents. Like the *Lady* she was still in wartime grey with one mast, the only concession to peacetime being her name painted in white on the bows. She was much in need of a major refit but her large capacity more than compensated for any lack of comfort.

The *Ben* was commanded until 27th March, 1946 by Captain Ratcliffe Duggan. He was the oldest Captain ever to serve Calais, having been born six months earlier than Captain Woods, in June, 1879. He joined the Company in 1907 and at the outbreak of war was in command of the *Mona's Queen*. This ship, after evacuating troops and civilians from Rotterdam and Boulogne, subsequently struck a magnetic mine and sank off Dunkirk. Captain Duggan was awarded the D.S.C., and was six times Mentioned in Despatches. He subsequently commanded the *Ben-My-Chree* in the North Sea, at Normandy and during her trooping service to Ostend and Calais until his retirement three months before his 68th birthday. He died in April, 1957 aged 77 years.

During the brief period that the *Lady* and the *Ben* both served the Calais route together, we were somewhat apprehensive if one ship was scheduled to be first out of Calais and the other first out of Dover if the wind was blowing a full gale. Although both the elderly Manxmen knew the Channel like the back of their hands, it would have been only natural for them to contact each other by radio telephone before deciding whether to hazard their vessels in bad weather particularly as they knew that both they and their ships were shortly to be demobilized. But they did not fail the Army.

Captain Duggan was succeeded by Captain J. Walter Cubbon. Born in 1890, he joined the Company in 1920 and was in command of the *Fenella* when that ship was sunk at Dunkirk. She was hit by dive bombers and lumps of concrete from the quay. Personnel on board were transferred to the General Steam Navigation paddle steamer *Crested Eagle* but this ship too was bombed and set on fire almost immediately; sixteen of the *Fenella*'s crew being lost.

Captain Cubbon was also one of the various Masters to command the *Victoria* between the invasion of Normandy and the end of the war. It fell to him to bring the *Ben* back to the Mersey on 11th May, 1946. He remained as her Captain and was Commodore of the fleet until his retirement in January, 1955. He died in July, 1977 aged 87.

Captain W.E. McMeiken, Commodore of the Company until his retirement in 1972, served as Chief Officer of the *Ben* during her time on the Dover – Calais run. In a letter full of fascinating memories, he has given me much help on the personnel serving on the Manx ships (see *Victoria*).

To come back to the *Ben*, despite the poor condition in which she was returned, Cammell Laird managed to have her ready for peacetime service in six weeks. She had a much more thorough refit in the winter of 1946/47. Following the completion of four new ships between 1946 and 1948, the *Ben* became a summer season only ship running from Liverpool or Fleetwood. Her comfortable accommodation and spacious capacity made her a popular ship to the end. She was finally withdrawn in 1965 and given the suffix II following the launch of the new car ferry *Ben-My-Chree*. Eventually in December, 1965 she was towed from Birkenhead to be broken up at Bruges.

Chapter 12
Victoria (Code No.PH78)

The *Victoria* was in many ways an unique ship to operate on the Calais trooping route. She was built in 1907 and sometimes looked as though she belonged to an earlier age. The *Manxman* was even older (built in 1904) but she did not appear until August, 1946. The *Victoria*, the smallest of the ships, with her tall masts and funnels and belching clouds of oil smoke could not be mistaken. She was part of the Dover/Folkestone – Calais scene for 22 months and next to *Biarritz* must have vied with *Royal Daffodil* for second place in the number of troops carried.

Victoria was no stranger to Calais. She was built in 1907 by Dennys of Dumbarton as one of a fleet of seven new turbine ships for the South Eastern and Chatham Railway to replace their paddle steamers. The first, the *Queen*, built in 1903 was lost during World War I. The second, the *Onward* became the *Mona's Isle* in 1920 and survived both wars. Her sister the *Invicta* was sold to the French in 1923 as was the *Victoria*'s sister, the *Empress*. Finally in 1911 the *Engadine* and *Riviera* appeared. The former was sold to Phillipine owners in 1933 and sunk in the Second World War. The latter was sold to Burns and Laird Lines in 1932, renamed *Laird's Isle* and ran on their Ardrossan – Belfast route until 1957 except for the war years. She too appeared briefly in Calais in January, 1945 on the Harwich route (see Chapter 15).

The *Victoria*, as built, had a gross tonnage of 1,641 tons and carried 1,536 passengers at a service speed of 22 knots, although, on one of her first crossings to Calais, she is reported to have broken all records by taking only 46 minutes.

Until World War I she served mainly on Dover – Calais but, with the arrival of the *Biarritz* and *Maid of Orleans* after the war she switched mainly to Folkestone – Boulogne. The transfer of ownership to the Southern Railway and the completion of the *Isle of Thanet* and *Maid of Kent* in 1925 made her a reserve ship and it was no surprise when she was sold to the Isle of Man Steam Packet Company in 1928 for only £25,000 though the cost after alterations was £37,550.

Victoria arriving Dover as troopship in April 1945. (Richard Danielson)

Victoria leaving Calais as troopship in July 1945.

The Isle of Man Company converted her to oil fuel in 1932/33 and she ran until the war, without major incident, on most of the Company's routes. Unlike the newer ships she was not initially requisitioned for trooping nor was she present at Dunkirk. In addition to maintaining the normal service, however, she had to transport numerous aliens interned on the Isle of Man.

However, it was in December, 1940 that she nearly met her end. The Merseyside air raids of that month included the laying of mines in the estuary. On 20th December, the *Victoria* exploded two but reached port unscathed. On 27th December, however, when outward bound with a large number of passengers, she exploded another mine eight miles North West of the Bar Lightship. Her passengers were taken off by the trawler *Michael Griffiths* while H.M.Y. *Evadne* stood by. The stricken ship was towed back to the Mersey for repairs. She did not return to the Island service but was used as a target vessel for the Fleet Air Arm in the Firth of Forth, though still under the Red Ensign, until her conversion to a Landing Ship Infantry (Hand Hoisting) at the end of 1943 at Leith. As such, like the majority of the ships in this story, she was present at Normandy on D-Day as part of Force 'J'. She had the distinction of loading 47 Royal Marine Commando at Southampton. This unit, breaking out westward from Arromanches towards the U.S. sector, captured Port-en-Bessin. *Victoria* sailed again from Weymouth on D + 3 in company with the *Canterbury*. From then until January, 1945 she worked out of Southampton, Portsmouth or Newhaven to Arromanches, Cherbourg or Dieppe. In March, 1945 she became part of the South East Coast Ports Pool.

The *Victoria*'s first appearance in Calais was on 2nd April, 1945. She ran in tandem with *Isle of Guernsey* for three weeks from Newhaven carrying 750 troops. The service was only intended to be temporary while No.1 berth at Folkestone was being dredged. After this she ran regularly from Dover or Folkestone to Calais carrying 1,500 troops until her release in February, 1947.

As indicated in the first paragraph, her appearance was unmistakeable. On a clear day we always knew when the *Victoria* was on her way by the billow of smoke in the Straits. Nor inevitably was her accommodation de luxe. The senior officers, who came down from HQ BAOR on the Rhine Army special train, crossed on the first ship at about 8.30 am. If this was the *Victoria* they were somewhat surprised, on enquiring about cabins or the officers' saloon, to be told

Victoria off Calais arriving light from Dover in August 1946.   (Keith Lewis)

Victoria off Douglas in her peacetime role in 1950.   (John Hendy)

that space was reserved for them on the open boat deck under the bridge. To be fair the Generals took this in good part. Less senior officers could be more difficult but even they were not inclined to wait for a later if less spartan ship.

Because it was known that she would be retained for sometime, the *Victoria* was the first ship to appear in Calais in peacetime Isle of Man colours in the spring of 1946. The single black iron hoops on the red funnels with black tops gave her the appearance of an elderly miniature Cunarder. They may have been a survival of bolts to sections of the funnels from her early days in the Straits as they differed from the hoops on the other ships. Her accommodation was also improved so that she was among the first ships (with *Prince Charles*) to carry wives and families to Italy in April, 1946. Folkestone was re-opened specially to the military for this purpose. Some of this structural alteration was in fact carried out while she was still in service once the war ended.

Inevitably there were minor incidents. On 11th May, 1945 she struck the breakwater entering Calais, damaged her starboard quarter and propellor blades and had to retire to Tilbury for repairs. Other minor engine repairs saw her off service briefly later in the year. My records show, however, that there were only two months out of the 22 she served when she did not sail regularly.

Her long stint on the Calais route was eventually ended by another Isle of Man Steamer, the *Manxman*, which had first arrived on the service in late August, 1946. On the return of the *Manxman* from a spell of duty at Harwich on 2nd March, 1947 the *Vic* at last left for Birkenhead having been released by the Ministry of Transport.

The records show that the *Victoria* had three Masters during her time on the Calais route. Captain J. Keig served briefly, initially, but died in February, 1946 aged only 53.

Captain G.R. Kinley took over the ship in her last months at Calais from 4th October, 1946 and is still alive aged 84.

But the Captain who commanded the ship for the bulk of her service on the Calais route was Captain P.J. ('Ginger') Bridson. Born in 1893 he joined the Isle Man Steam Packet Company in 1913 and served during the First War. By 1945 the red hair (and freckled face) which gave him his nickname had gone rather thin on top but he was a fit, friendly man and very helpful to the Army. Concrete evidence of this is to be found in the fact that he refereed an Army football match in Calais on Christmas Day, 1945 when the *Victoria* was having a well deserved rest.

Captain Bridson came to the *Victoria* from the *Viking*, an even older ship, and had a distinguished eleven years with the Company after the war. His first peacetime command was the Company's second post-war ship *Mona's Queen* which sailed on her maiden voyage from Liverpool to Douglas on 26th June, 1946. Subsequently he commanded the *Snaefell*. His final command was the sixth and last classic (i.e. non car ferry) ship to be built for the Company, the 1955 *Manxman* now withdrawn from service and laid up at Preston. Captain Bridson retired on his 65th birthday on 30th June, 1958. He died on 26th September, 1964.

Both Captain Bridson and Captain Kinley were subsequently Commodores of the Isle of Man Fleet as was Captain McMeiken, Chief Officer of the *Ben-My-Chree* when she was based at Dover. He tells me that 'Ned' Gelling was Chief Officer of the *Vic* at the time and her Chief Engineer was 'Spinks' Cain.

The *Victoria*, after a limited refit by Cammell Laird, actually managed to appear for the 1947 season. Her winters were spent laid up at the Tongue in Douglas Harbour. She sailed on until the end of the 1956 season when she entered Wallasey Dock, Birkenhead. From there she was towed to Barrow-in-Furness by the Liverpool tug *Rosegarth* on 25th January, 1957. Like the *Viking* she spent 49 years in service but was 50 years old by the time she was broken up. This would appear to be a record for a cross channel passenger ship continuously under British ownership.

Chapter 13
Manxman

The *Manxman* was the last troopship to arrive on the Calais scene as late as the end of August, 1946. She also formally closed the route running the last regular trooping sailing on 1st August, 1947. After this, except for an occasional charter, any troops on the route travelled on the civilian crossing.

The *Manxman* also had the distinction of being the oldest ship on the route, having been built by Vickers at Barrow in 1904, three years before the *Victoria*. She and her three sisters were designed by Sir John Biles for the Midland Railway. Her initial gross tonnage was 2,174 tons, later reduced to 2,030. Dimensions were 341' (overall length), 43.1' beam and 17.3' depth; she had three overall decks and carried 2,010 passengers in two classes. With triple screws, her Parsons turbines produced a speed of 22 knots. Whilst her sisters ran from Heysham to Belfast, she inaugurated the Heysham – Douglas run, hence her name.

Requisitioned on the outbreak of the first war, the *Manxman* was purchased outright by the Admiralty in 1915 and became a seaplane carrier with hangars fore and aft of the funnels. Like the *Ben-My-Chree* (III) she served in the Mediterranean.

In 1920 she was purchased by the Isle of Man Steam Packet Company, the name being appropriate. Her bulwarks forward were retained, the forepart below the boat deck was plated in and the boat deck itself extended by being joined to the short deck around the mainmast. As the largest ship in the fleet, she ran from Liverpool to Douglas as the flagship until the arrival of the *Ben-My-Chree* (IV) in 1927. She was converted to burn oil fuel as early as 1921. In the 1930s as the new ships arrived she ran mainly from Douglas to Dublin or Belfast.

She was again requisitioned immediately on the outbreak of the Second World War and served as a troopship to France. She made only two voyages to Dunkirk rescuing 2,394 men, but her finest hour came later in June, 1940. Under Captain P.B. Cowley, she made several crossings, initially to Le Havre, and finally was the last troopship out of Cherbourg. With tanks approaching the quay and cranes blown into the water, the 'cheeky two funnel steamer', as Rommel

Manxman off Douglas before the war.   (John Clarkson)

Manxman at Preston at the end of her trooping service in 1949.   (John Clarkson)

described her, left crowded with troops and escorted by a destroyer. She was also the last ship out of St Malo.

There was something of an anti-climax after this. 1941 found her laid up at the Tongue at Douglas. However, the Admiralty had established a Radio and Direction Finding (Radar) base at Douglas. Initially two yachts were used for sea training but, in October, 1941, the *Manxman* again found herself under the White Ensign as H.M.S. *Caduceus*. The Southern Railway *Isle of Sark* and the former French minelayer *Pollux* completed the flotilla. The ratings under training must have appreciated the improved sea keeping qualities of their 'new' ships. Nevertheless, under R.N. command, the *Manxman* twice collided with the Victoria Pier in Douglas which led to suggestions that the Admiralty might have given temporary commissions to Steam Packet Company Masters. Doubtless to achieve calmer conditions, the flotilla moved to the Clyde in 1943 and here the ship remained for over two years training thousands of ratings for the Fleet.

She was not decommissioned until late 1945 when she was refitted as a troopship. Her bridge was considerably built up and plated in forward and larger lifeboats were fitted with four sets of deck-pivoted gravity davits. Four large embarkation doors were cut on each side of her long deckhouse ('promenade deck') beneath the boat deck to speed up embarkation of troops. She was also one of the few troopships to have radar. This refit meant that her interior was less spartan than those of some of the ships.

She served on the Tilbury – Ostend run in early 1946 but the latter port was closed in March. She did not appear in Calais until late August, 1946. She spent the early summer helping out on Harwich – Hook. When she did arrive in Calais, like the *Victoria*, her profile was from another (Edwardian) age but, painted in Isle of Man Steam Packet Company colours, she still retained much of her original elegance. The more solidly built bridge with the foremast rising from the structure aft of the wheelhouse was offset by the counter stern, tall thin funnels and long low lines.

She served Calais continuously until 14th February, 1947 when she left for a two week stint at Harwich leaving the *Victoria* to maintain the trooping service on her own until 22nd February when the *Biarritz* returned from refit to Greenock. The *Manxman* returned from Harwich on 2nd March thus releasing the *Victoria*.

The *Biarritz* made her last crossing to Calais on 7th July and the *Manxman* formally ended the service on 1st August, 1947 and left for Harwich. She was really too small, and larger ships were available anyway, for the regular trooping service from Harwich to the Hook. But for 18 months she performed valuable service in the movement of German prisoners of war from the U.K. and displaced persons to and from the U.K. who required resettlement in the aftermath of the Second World War. Captain Griffin, subsequently Marine Superintendent of the Company, recalls that the Germans were very disciplined but the return voyages were not always so pleasant. She may in fact have already initiated this service in the summer of 1946 and she certainly operated from Tilbury in June, 1947 when the *Biarritz* served Calais alone.

By February, 1949, however, the ship was worn out and no longer required. She arrived at Barrow from Harwich on 28th February, having sheltered en route in Ramsey Bay. On August 9th she was towed from Barrow to Preston for scrapping.

During her time at Calais the regular Master of the *Manxman* was Captain Oscar Taylor. Born in 1892, he joined the Isle of Man Steam Packet Company in 1912. He was in command of the *Tynwald* (IV) after Dunkirk during the evacuation of the Western French ports following which the ship was used to transport German prisoners of war from Liverpool to the 'Tail of the Bank' on the Clyde where they were transferred to troopships bound for Canada. Appropriately Captain Taylor was in command of the *Tynwald* (V) on her maiden voyage to Douglas on 31st July, 1947. He returned to the *Manxman*, however, to take her on her last voyage from Harwich to Barrow. He retired in 1957 and died in 1972 at the age of 79.

Chapter 14
General Steam Navigation Co. Ltd

M.V. *Royal Daffodil*

The *Royal Daffodil* was unique in various respects among the Calais fleet. First she was the only diesel engined vessel. Now there are no steam turbine cross channel ships. Secondly, she was the only one of the passenger ships not present at Normandy. Thirdly, it must be a moot point whether she or the *Victoria* won second place to the *Biarritz* for making the most crossings as troopships between Dover/Folkestone and Calais because they both joined and left the route at approximately the same time.

Her name requires some explanation. In preparation for the raid on Zeebrugge on 23rd April, 1918, the Royal Navy requisitioned two Mersey ferries *Daffodil* and *Iris*, their main purpose being to hold H.M.S. *Vindictive* alongside the mole. Both ships did valiant work and both survived, though with many casualties. King George Vth therefore decreed that the prefix *Royal* should be added to the name of each ship. The *Daffodil* was purchased by Captain S.J. Shippick of the New Medway Steam Packet Co. Ltd in 1934 to run cruises on the Medway and in the Thames docks. She was really too slow for this work, however, and was scrapped in 1938.

By this time the New Medway Steam Packet Co. had been absorbed by the General Steam Navigation Co. so the name, as it were, passed into their hands. Before the merger, Captain Shippick had already ordered, in 1935, from Dennys of Dumbarton a diesel engined ship for day excursions from the Thames and Kent resorts to France to supplement the services run since 1928 by the paddle steamers *Queen of Kent* and *Queen of Thanet* both converted First War minesweepers. The diesel ship *Queen of the Channel*, 1,162 tons, proved so successful that a larger version *Royal Sovereign*, 1,527 tons, came into service in 1937 and a still larger ship *Royal Daffodil* in June, 1939. Her tonnage was 2,060 gross tons and her speed 21 knots with a passenger capacity also of 2,060, to the Kent and Essex coasts, and 1,392 for cross channel excursions from Tilbury/Gravesend to Southend, Margate and either Calais, Boulogne or Ostend. The boat deck did not span the full breadth of

Royal Daffodil arriving at Dover from Calais on VE Day 1945. The strong sun makes the grey hull look white as it was in peacetime.   (Captain Conway)

the ship so that four gangways could be lowered onto the open promenade deck on the port or starboard side. *Queen of the Channel* was
lost at Dunkirk and *Royal Sovereign* was mined and sunk off Barry
in December, 1940.

There was some resentment on Merseyside at the retention of the
name *Royal Daffodil* by the London company but, as will be
recorded, by the end of her war service, she was a ship in which all
could take pride.

Royal Daffodil's war work started on 1st September, 1939 when
for three days she evacuated London school children from London
to Norfolk, disembarking them at Lowestoft. After this she served as
a troopship between Dover or Southampton and France.

Her finest hour, however, came in May, 1940. On the evening of
22nd May she embarked the 2nd Battalion the 60th Rifles (The
King's Royal Rifle Corps) and, after joining a convoy at Dover, disembarked them at the Quai Gare Maritime at Calais the next morning. Sadly, after fighting for four days all were killed or captured
except for a few brought out by the Royal Navy on the night of 26th

78

Royal Daffodil alongside at Calais in July 1945.

May. The 60th were particularly active in defence of the Gare Maritime area.

Thus *Royal Daffodil* was already available at Dover when the evacuation from Dunkirk began in earnest on the evening of 26th May and left Dover in convoy by the longer route; the shorter route via Gravelines being under shellfire from the shore. After surviving heavy bombing in the harbour she brought 950 men home to Dover. On 28th May again in daylight she evacuated 1,800 men to Margate. On 29th May she was back again — estimated load varies between 750 and 1,700. All sources agree that on 30th May she brought over 2,000 French troops back to Dover. After difficulties on 31st May she was back again in daylight on the morning of 1st June and brought back nearly another 2,000 French troops. It was, however, almost impossible for the ships to move in daylight by this time due to heavy bombing. *Royal Daffodil*'s final voyage on the evening of 2nd June nearly proved her last. Five of six bombs aimed at her fell clear but the sixth hit the ship, passed through three decks into the engine room and went out through the starboard side before exploding just clear of the ship. She began to make water through the hole so the port boats were lowered to the deck and filled with water to

79

February 1947. *Royal Daffodil* is demobilised at last in the Thames (Deptford Creek).
(Topham Photo Library)

correct the list. This raised the starboard side enough to lift the hole clear of the water line.

Mr J. Coulthard, the Chief Engineer, and Mr W. Evans, Second Engineer, plugged the hole with beds and kept the pumps going so the ship limped back to Ramsgate, with the engines running very slowly on a mixture of 3 parts water to 1 of oil, and landed those troops she had been able to pick up before the bombing. It is impossible to be precise but all told *Royal Daffodil* brought over 8,000 troops back from Dunkirk. She anchored off Ramsgate and was assisted by the salvage vessel *Forde* from Deal. The tugs *Lady Brassey* (Dover Harbour Board) and *Doria* towed her to Dover where she was beached. If the weather had been unkind she might have sunk. In the event she proceeded without assistance on 3rd June to the London Docks for repairs.

Her work was recognized by the award of the D.S.C. to her Master, Captain George Johnson, her Chief Officer, Mr A. Patrick (Pat) J. Paterson, who was to relieve Captain Johnson as Master while she was on the Calais run in 1945, and Mr Coulthard, the Chief Engineer. The D.S.M. went to Donkeyman Albert Delmain and Mr Evans, Second Engineer, and Mr Woodhouse, Second Officer, were

Mentioned in Despatches. Except for the Isle of Man steamer *Tynwald* this was the largest number of awards received by any personnel ship.

The damage suffered at Dunkirk meant that the ship played no further part in the evacuations from France after Dunkirk. September, 1940 however found her trooping at Stranraer, the port on the south west tip of Scotland. This was to be her base for 4½ years.

Until the end of 1943 she ran to Larne as a troopship. But on 3rd January, 1944 she became the official mail ship, on charter to the London, Midlands and Scottish Railway, until 24th December, while *Princess Margaret* was away as a Landing Ship Infantry for Normandy. *Royal Daffodil* remained at Stranraer as a troopship until March, 1945 when *Duchess of Hamilton* from the Clyde joined P & A Campbell's *Empress Queen* on the trooping run.

There were two reasons why she was not utilized as a Landing Ship. First, like her two earlier smaller sisters, she was built with a deliberate bulge amidships rather like a modified sponson on a paddle steamer. This made her breadth at its widest point seven feet greater than the *Canterbury*. This, together with the inset boat deck already mentioned, would have made the carriage of Landing Craft even slung outboard extremely difficult. The position of her lifeboats illustrates the point. Although four were on the boat deck and two right at the stern on the promenade deck, all were well aft of the midships area.

The second reason is that she had a much shallower draft (only 8'9") than a normal cross channel ship as she was designed to berth at Margate Pier at low water. Although entirely seaworthy, she was undeniably tender in rough weather.

The *Royal Daffodil* arrived at Dover from Portsmouth on 9th April, 1945 and commenced sailings to Calais on 11th April. From then on, apart from occasional diversions to Ostend in the early months, she remained permanently on the run until her release in January, 1947 except for one period. Apart from the usual problems caused by minor mechanical defects, her stay was singularly free of incident. Although the war had taken its toll, the fact that she was only completed in June, 1939 meant that she was free from some of the mechanical defects of the older ships. It would have been incongruous to paint her hull in its peacetime white at this stage whilst her normal buff funnel colours would have contrasted oddly with the grey hull. As already indicated she was an easy ship to turn round quickly.

Royal Daffodil off Deal Pier in 1950. (John Hendy)

One incident, which might have been more serious, was when Captain Johnson signalled that an exuberant Canadian, being demobilized had let off a grenade in one of the pedestals of the men's lavatories. Damage was fortunately slight.

Christmas and New Year's Eve, 1945 were not happy times for the ship, however. It had been agreed that only compassionate cases would be carried over Christmas on one ship. The *Lady of Mann*'s sailing was cancelled due to adverse weather on Christmas Eve. On Christmas Day the *Royal Daffodil* set off for Folkestone as it had been decided that naval and military and railway staff at Dover would operate on Christmas Eve and Boxing Day but take a well earned day off on Christmas Day. Unfortunately there was still a south easterly gale blowing (the worst wind direction for berthing at Folkestone) and the ship had to return. The *Invicta* took the passengers, originally intended for both the 24th and 25th December sailings, on Boxing Day. I record the incident because it was reported at the time in the press and Questions were subsequently asked in the House of Commons. Unfortunate as it may have been for the personnel involved it would obviously have been wrong to hazard the ship.

On New Year's Eve, in company with the *Lady of Mann* (ex Dover), the *Royal Daffodil* was fogbound off Calais for the night when making the last sailing of the day from Folkestone. In this case the returning troops merely exchanged one boring New Year's Eve for another, as, had they disembarked, they would have been on a train all night on the way back to their units.

Captain Wilf Conway, who was Second Officer of the *Royal Daffodil* at this time, recalls that the ship was on the Newhaven – Dieppe run from February to April, 1946. Unusually we had sufficient ships for Calais (see Chapter 3). *Royal Daffodil* relieved in turn *Isle of Thanet, Isle of Guernsey* and *Worthing* which were running a mixed civilian/trooping service. By this time the civilian service was mainly run by the *Worthing* (ex H.M.S. *Brigadier*) as the *Daffodil* was not equipped for civilian passengers. Until the reopening of the 'Golden Arrow', Newhaven – Dieppe was the only route for non-service personnel to France.

Except for the above diversion and periodic refits *Royal Daffodil* remained on the route until January, 1947. She and the *Victoria* were the last ships out of Folkestone before that port was handed back to the Southern Railway for civilian traffic on 10th March, 1946. By the time she was demobilized she had steamed 170,000 miles for the Ministry of War Transport and carried 2,443,979 service and civilian passengers.

Until November, 1945 *Royal Daffodil* was commanded by Captain George Johnson, D.S.C. who had been her Master since she first came into service in 1939. Mr Peter Pole, now living in the Shetlands, who served on the ship in her first year, recalls that they received a warning in the summer of 1939 that the I.R.A. were going to bomb the ship as she passed under Tower Bridge. Fortunately it proved a false alarm; but it is right to remember the campaign of the I.R.A. in the late 1930s. The crew came mainly from Norfolk, and of Captain Johnson, Mr Pole says 'He was a fine man, apart from being an excellent Captain'. I recall him as a bluff, friendly character.

Born in 1900 he joined the General Steam Navigation Co. in 1921. After leaving *Royal Daffodil* he commanded the *Empire Parkeston*. She was the former Canadian West Coast Ship *Prince Henry* and by then had become one of the three regular troopships on the Harwich – Hook route, the others being the *Vienna* and *Empire Wansbeck* (ex *Linz*). In the summer of 1948 he took command of the new *Royal Sovereign*. This lasted for four seasons. He resigned in 1951 and joined the Amsterdam Dry Dock Co. He died in February, 1978. As his brother, Gerald Johnson, says 'A Master Mariner par excellence'.

Captain Johnson was succeeded as Master by Captain A.P. (Pat) Paterson, D.S.C. Born in 1904, he joined the G.S.N. in 1936 and served as Chief Officer on *Royal Daffodil* from the start of her career. He seemed a fairly quiet character but Mr John Pover, retired Chief Engineer of the P & O Dover – Boulogne cross channel ships, has filled out the details for me. In later years he was known as a jovial, robust fun lover who drove a white Daimler when ashore! He remained in command of *Royal Daffodil* until 1953 and added the M.B.E. to his D.S.C., in 1951. He subsequently commanded the *Empire Parkeston* in the Suez expedition and was Master of the G.S.N. cargo ship *Tern* when she was trading on the Miami – Ecuador, and subsequently the Russian route in the 1950s. He died suddenly in his sleep on 5th January, 1963 whilst still serving with the Company. The G.S.N. News Letter records that 'he was known to almost everybody in the G.S.N. and to very many outside the Company'.

Royal Daffodil had a major reconversion at Dennys in 1947 which was completed at the New Medway Steam Packet Co.'s yard at Acorn Wharf on the Medway at Rochester. Her life was somewhat frustrated until 1955 as 'no passport' day excursions to the Continent were forbidden by Government regulations; so she could only cruise off the French coast. But from 1955 until 1966 she resumed excursions to Calais, Boulogne and Ostend from her nightly base at Gravesend (West) Pier and Tilbury. I did not realise, when I saw her in Boulogne on 14th September, 1966 that this was to be her last commercial voyage. In December, 1966 the General Steam Navigation Co. announced that the growth of car and coach traffic by other routes had caused the popularity of their day trips to wane and terminated the service.

The two post war ships *Royal Sovereign* and *Queen of the Channel* eventually found other owners but *Royal Daffodil* sailed in February, 1967 from the South West India Docks in London to Ghent in Belgium under the command of her last Master, Captain Peter Stoddart. A crew member at the time said that 'her engines were good for another twenty years'. As John Pover says: 'They were indeed as they were Sulzer engines, the Rolls Royce of the Marine side'. Paradoxically the growth of day trippers, since they were allowed to bring back duty free goods, has caused some discomfort to car and lorry passengers on the cross channel ships. So *Royal Daffodil* and her consorts, were they still available, could have found a role. In any event it is twenty years too late for *Royal Daffodil*.

Chapter 15
Burns and Laird Line Ltd

Laird's Isle

The *Laird's Isle* only came to Calais three times when she ran on the Harwich service in January, 1945. But she is worth more than a passing mention because, like the *Victoria*, Calais had been a familiar port to her in her earlier career — from 1911 – 1932.

She was built by Dennys (Yard Number No.937) for the South Eastern and Chatham Railway's Dover – Calais and Folkestone – Boulogne services. Launched on 1st April, 1911, she was named *Riviera* by Miss Bonsor, daughter of the Chairman of the Company. Her gross tonnage was 1,929 tons. She and her sister the *Engadine* were the sixth and seventh, and last, of the new generation of triple screws and powered by three direct Parsons steam turbines, the slightly additional horse power of this pair of ships enabled them to maintain a service speed of 23 knots and thus cut the Dover – Calais crossing to one hour.

The two ships were requisitioned on the outbreak of the First War and served as seaplane carriers for the Royal Naval Air Service operating off enemy coasts in the North Sea.

The *Riviera* was refitted in Chatham Dockyard and reopened the Folkestone – Boulogne service in April, 1920. The accompanying photo shows her leaving Boulogne in the early 1920s in South Eastern and Chatham Railway colours. The *Riviera* was destined to survive longer than the Casino and other buildings seen in the background and on the skyline of Boulogne, all of which were destroyed during the Second World War. The picture does show the ship's clean lines and elegant appearance although, at this stage, the promenade deck was not plated in. On transfer to the Southern Railway in 1923 the black funnels became buff with black top.

The *Biarritz* and *Maid of Orleans* had already displaced the *Riviera* and *Engadine* on the Dover – Calais run and, when the former were in turn displaced by the *Isle of Thanet* and *Maid of Kent*, the *Riviera* became a relief ship and was also used in summer for day excursions. As such, however, she remained in the Straits until the end of 1932

Laird's Isle in South Eastern and Chatham Railway colours at Boulogne in 1923. Nearly all the buildings in the background were destroyed in the war.

when she was sold to a Mr J.B. Couper of Glasgow, reputedly for only £5,000 and promptly resold to Burns and Laird Lines.

Her new owners renamed her *Laird's Isle* and the ship underwent extensive renovation at Ardrossan including conversion to an oil burner. She opened the daylight service to Belfast on 16th June, 1933 running daily during the summer months except on Sundays when she offered coastal cruises. Her passenger capacity was 1,250 (plus 57 crew) of which 700 were saloon and 550 second class.

On the outbreak of war in September, 1939 she was again requisitioned, serving initially as an armed boarding vessel stopping and searching neutral ships for contraband. She is not listed as being present at Dunkirk and her service until 1943 was mainly in Northern waters partly as a training ship and protecting convoys. However, like most of her contemporaries, she was converted in the winter of 1943/44 to a Landing Ship Infantry (Hand Hoisting) (Code No.PH68) and joined Force 'J'. She landed U.S. troops on D-Day but then sailed from Newhaven on D + 3, in company with the *Isle of Guernsey* with British troops. After this she reverted to the U.S. sector operating out of Southampton and Weymouth.

Laird's Isle as troopship in Southampton in 1946. (John Pover)

However, 5th January, 1945 found her off Calais. She entered the harbour at the second attempt due to weather and embarked 500 troops for Harwich. She sailed again for Harwich on 9th and 11th January. However, the ship had had no proper refit since D-Day and, not surprisingly, broke down in Harwich on 13th January and had to be sent to North Shields for two months. She reappeared on the Tilbury – Ostend service on 5th March but luck was against her as she damaged her bows on 15th March when she struck the breakwater at Ostend. Mr Pover, who has already appeared in this narrative in the chapter on the *Royal Daffodil*, joined her in the London Docks at this time. After proceeding via Dover in convoy to Southampton, she was based on the latter port until 9th January, 1946 carrying U.S. troops to Le Havre or Cherbourg (see photo). Her Master was Captain Jackson and her Chief Engineer, Mr Morrison. After 35 years, John Pover still found her the fastest ship in the Channel and her three turbines 'could use all the steam you could give them'.

The *Laird's Isle* was released in January, 1946, after storm damage, and despite her age, was installed with entirely new public rooms. The forward end of her promenade deck was plated in and fitted with large windows. She retained a naval siren as a reminder of her war activities which was used in preference to her more subdued civilian whistle. The ship made her first post-war crossing on 29th July, 1946 and resumed her pre-war routine.

For the next eleven years, the *Laird's Isle* maintained the summer service regularly until August 6th, 1957 when she made her last sailing from Belfast to Ardrossan. She was laid up at Greenock and left there on October 9th, 1957 to be broken up at Troon.

At the age of 46, she was the seventh ship in this story to last forty years or more. Now, running round the clock with three crews, cross channel ships are lucky to achieve twenty years.

Chapter 16
Belgian Marine Administration

Prinses Astrid (Code No.PS85)
Prince Charles (Code No.PS87)
Prinses Josephine Charlotte (Code No.PS88)

All nine ships of the Belgian Marine escaped from the Germans in 1940. The newest ship *Prince Phillipe* arrived with only one engine installed. She was sunk in collision in the Irish Sea in July, 1941. The *Prince Leopold* was mined and sunk south east of the Nab Tower, off Bembridge, Isle of Wight, while on passage from Normandy on 29th July, 1944.

This chapter is concerned with the three ships which served Calais, f briefly, between January, 1945 and April, 1946. The names may :ause confusion. In peacetime, the Belgian ships were named alternately in Flemish and French. All the nine ships which came to the U.K. flew the White Ensign during the war and their names were anglicised accordingly. This will account for the change in spelling in the narrative.

The three ships noted at the head of this chapter (plus *Prince Leopold*) were launched between 1929 and 1931. Built by Cockerills of Hoboken with a gross tonnage of 2938/3088 and a steam horse power of 13,500, they were considerably larger than any previous ships on the route and had a service speed of 24 knots. Their high superstructure forward — the bridge rose three levels above the promenade deck — gave them an unusual appearance in that the funnels were only marginally higher than the wheelhouse. To me, however, they were handsome ships. At least I thought so when I crossed on the *Leopold* and returned on the *Charles* in 1937.

The ships pursued a normal life until the war. Limited crossings were maintained until May, 1940 but none of them was involved in Dunkirk although they did transport refugees. After the collapse of France, it was at first intended to convert the three with which this chapter is concerned into hospital ships. The Admiralty suddenly realised, however, that these vessels were considerably faster than any other cross channel ships except for those on the Newhaven – Dieppe route. All of these had been lost or held in French ports

Prinses Astrid in peacetime before the war.

except for the *Worthing* (H.M.S. *Brigadier*). *Astrid* and *P.J.C.* (*Josephine-Charlotte*) were therefore converted at Silley Cox & Co., Falmouth and *Charles* at Devonport Dockyard (with *Leopold*) into Landing Ships Infantry (L.S.I.(S)) earmarked for special duties as Combined Operations ships. As such they carried eight Landing Craft Assault (compared with six for the merchant ships converted in 1943) slung inboard on gravity hoists, and much of their superstructure was cut away (see photos).

Sadly, in view of language problems, it was decided that their Belgian crews could not remain with them, except for a limited number of engine room staff. All three ships emerged in 1941 as H.M.S. *Princess Astrid*, H.M.S. *Princess* Josephine Charlotte and H.M.S. *Prince Charles*.

After a few Norwegian sorties, all three ships were prepared for Dieppe. However, the *Astrid* and the *P.J.C.* were bombed in Yarmouth (Isle of Wight) Roads on 7th July, 1942. The Dieppe operation was originally scheduled for July. *Astrid* escaped fairly lightly but a bomb which exploded beneath the hull of *P.J.C.* caused severe damage and put her out of action for a year. *Astrid*, however, took the Royal Regiment of Canada to Dieppe on 19th August, 1942 and *Charles* sailed from Southampton with the Essex Scottish of Canada.

Both ships were joined by *P.J.C.* for the invasions at Sicily and Salerno. For the most part they carried Commandos and were therefore present at the start of each landing.

All the Belgians were back in U.K. waters in time for Normandy and sailed as part of Force 'J4'. *Astrid* carried No.4 Commando (326 men) to Ouistreham. *P.J.C.* took the first load of No.47 Commando (see also *Victoria*) and *Charles* landed U.S. Rangers on Omaha Beach. The ships sailed either from Southampton or Weymouth and there were the customary follow up landings.

It has taken a long time to bring the Belgians into the Calais story and we must now split the history of the ships accordingly.

1 (a) **H.M.S.** *Princess Astrid*

The *Astrid* first appeared in Calais in January, 1945 on the Harwich run. The ships were only allowed to carry 500 troops and usually sailed overnight to avoid the danger from E-boats and submarines operating from Dutch ports. *Astrid* was unable to cross to Calais on the night of 18/19th January owing to fog and anchored in the Downs.

A more serious episode occurred on 12th February when the *Astrid* fouled an obstruction at the entrance to Calais, having been blown off course by the wind. Her stern was holed and she began to settle down aft. It was, however, possible to disembark the troops. Fortunately she did not block the harbour and, after a week's patching up of the damage, left for Southampton for repairs which took four months. During this period her landing craft hoists were removed, her dazzle camouflage changed to uniform grey and some of her superstructure was restored. More important she was decommissioned by the Royal Navy and reappeared, eventually, on the Dover/Tilbury – Ostend run in July 1945 with a Belgian crew.

Prinses Astrid as Landing Ship Infantry, H.M.S. *Princess Astrid* (minus landing craft).
(Public Record Office)

H.M.S. *Princess Josephine Charlotte* as Landing Ship Infantry.   (Imperial War Museum)

(b) *Prinses Astrid*

To our surprise the *Astrid* reappeared in Calais in January, 1946 at the time when sailings to Ostend were being run down. Dover had warned us that she was in poor shape and having trouble with her engines, but, to my amazement, when crossing on the *Lady of Mann* on 20th January, 1946, the *Astrid* which had left Calais nearly thirty minutes after us, appeared off Dover challenging for the Eastern entrance. Having already travelled on the *Lady* four times, I wished I had risked the *Astrid* to see what she was really like at this time.

She was commanded by Captain Kesterloot. She was finally handed back to the Belgian Government on 16th February, 1946 and ran on the civilian service from 1947. However, ill fated to the last, like the gracious lady who launched her in 1929, she struck a mine in Dunkirk Roads while on passage to Dover on 21st June, 1949. Five of her engine room crew were killed but the 218 passengers were safely taken to Dunkirk by other vessels. Ten minutes later the ship sank. Although her masts and funnels remained above the water, she resisted salvage attempts and broke her back on 26th June.

The Belgian tribute to their 'beloved' *Astrid* has been to name three further ships after her though it is a pity that the present holder of the name is an ex-Swedish vessel.

2 H.M.S. *Princess Josephine Charlotte*

The *P.J.C.* ran in company with the *Astrid* on the Harwich – Calais route in January/February, 1945. There were the customary delays due to fog but the *P.J.C.* made her last crossing on this route from Calais to Harwich on 25th February, 1945.

She never appeared again in Calais, but, while still under the White Ensign, took part in the liberation of the Channel Islands in May, 1945. After spending the summer of 1945 on the Dover – Ostend run she was finally handed back to the Belgians in October, 1945.

She relieved the *London – Istanbul* on the civilian Folkestone – Ostend route in May, 1946 and reopened the Dover – Ostend route in company with *Prince Baudouin* on 7th October, 1946.

Perhaps the bombing in 1942 had taken its toll as she was already in reserve by 1947 and was finally withdrawn on 26th November, 1950 and broken up at Boorn at the end of the year.

Prince Charles as Landing Ship Infantry, H.M.S. *Prince Charles*.   (Imperial War Museum)

Prince Charles as a troopship at Calais in March 1946.

Prince Charles as troopship leaving Calais in March 1946.

3 *Prince Charles*

The *Charles*, which incidentally holds the record of two hours 27 minutes for a peacetime crossing from Ostend to Dover, did not appear in Calais until the beginning of March, 1946.

She was damaged off Normandy in August, 1944 and released by the Royal Navy to the Ministry of War Transport in December, 1944. She subsequently ran as a troopship to Ostend from Dover/Tilbury.

The closure of Ostend in March, 1946 released her for Calais. In peacetime colours but with a stunted main mast, she was in good condition under the command of Captain Jansoome, whose son is currently writing a history of the wartime service of the Belgian ships.

The *Charles* took the first party of British service wives to Calais en route for Italy on 14th March, 1946. She was finally handed back to the Belgians on 15th June, 1946.

As a civilian ship she ran right through the 50s as the last Belgian turbine steamer, though latterly only in the summer. I have a picture of her laid up in Ostend in October, 1959. She was finally scrapped in 1961 in Belgium.

The Belgian fleet performed notable service in war and peace, none more so than the *lucky Albert* (H.M.S. *Prince Albert* & *Prins Albert*) which took part in every invasion including Southern France and the Far East. But there is no time to tell her story here as she never came to Calais.

95

Chapter 17
The Train Ferries

The *Shepperton Ferry* made history by being the first British merchant ship to enter Calais since May, 1940. When she arrived at the newly constructed Train Ferry berth (see Chapter 2) on 20th November, 1944 Lt. Col. George Wharton recalls that on the bridge were both Captain Kingsland, her Master at that time, and Captain Hancock, then Master of the *Twickenham Ferry* and Commodore of the pre-war Southern Railway Straits Fleet.

The two ships together with the *Hampton Ferry* had been ordered by the Southern Railway in 1934 from Swan Hunter and Wigham Richardson of Wallsend-on-Tyne. The Southern Railway had ambitious and well justified plans for the three ships. Unlike the Harwich – Zeebrugge train ferries which were cargo only, the new ships could accommodate 800 passengers and had a garage for 25 cars on the after end of the boat deck. Most important of all was the inception of the 'Night Ferry' sleeping car service which allowed passengers to occupy their train sleeper berths at Victoria Station in London and remain in their compartments until their arrival at the Gare du Nord in Paris the next morning. It would be idle to pretend that the journey was entirely silent, especially when the ship had to pass through the locks at Dunkirk, but it was a most comfortable way to travel particularly in good weather and was much used in its heyday by businessmen.

The service lasted except for the war years from 1936 to October, 1980. There was, however, a major initial hitch due to a delay in the completion of the Train Ferry dock at Dover. The three ships thus remained idle from early 1935 until October, 1936 mostly in Southampton. They are visible in various photos taken at the time of the maiden voyage of the *Queen Mary* in May, 1936. They were also periodically in the Wellington Dock at Dover. However, once the service started, it proved an immediate success for passengers and freight. The *Twickenham* was transferred to the French flag in March, 1939, though retaining Southern Railway colours. This was part of a complex arrangement with the Angleterre-Lorraine-Alsace S.A. de Navigation, whose four elderly ex-British passenger ships on the Folkestone – Dunkirk night route had been made redundant by the new service.

On 26th August, 1939 immediately prior to the outbreak of war, the *Hampton* and *Shepperton* were commissioned by the Royal Navy as H.M.S. *Hampton* and H.M.S. *Shepperton*, though largely retaining their Southern Railway crews; the former was under the command of Captain Payne (see *Invicta*). From 11th September, 1939 they were used as minelayers initially off Dover and Folkestone. With a capacity of 270 mines each, they were based on Dover. The *Shepperton* was released at Portsmouth in November, 1939 but the *Hampton* helped to lay the East Coast Barrier until May, 1940 and was not paid off at Portsmouth until July. The *Shepperton* was the last commercial ship out of Dunkirk when she brought back 2,500 refugees under command of the ever present Captain Walker (see *Canterbury*).

There is no record of the *Twickenham*'s activities at this time but it is worth noting that the three Harwich train ferries (TF1, TF2 and TF3) of the London and North Eastern Railway were switched on the Continental side from Zeebrugge to the old Calais Train Ferry berth at the town end of the Bassin Carnot. Their cargoes consisted of ambulance trains, rolling stock and heavy guns. This dock and, as noted in Chapter 2, the lock gates of the Bassin Carnot had all been destroyed by 1944.

Although the *Shepperton* assisted in the evacuation of the Channel Islands in June, 1940, she and the *Twickenham* were transferred to Stranraer and were joined by the *Hampton* in September. All three ships were now back under the Red Ensign with largely Southern Railway crews. They were able to use the ramps which had been built at Stranraer and Larne for the London, Midland and Scottish Railway's car ferry *Princess Victoria* built in 1939. This ship was lost in 1940; so the train ferries proved invaluable transporting military vehicles and at times other freight to and from Northern Ireland.

The *Hampton* left Stranraer in April, 1944 followed by the *Shepperton* and *Twickenham* in June to be fitted with overhanging gantries at the stern (see photo) and ramps, so that they could be used in the follow up to the invasion at French ports where dock facilities had been destroyed. They were thus able to commence a regular service from Southampton to Cherbourg in September, 1944. The derricks on the gantries could lift 84 tons and the ramps carried vehicles up to 60 tons.

Shepperton Ferry berthed at Calais in May 1945.

The two surviving Harwich train ferries now H.M.S. *Princess Iris* and H.M.S. *Daffodil* ran to Dieppe, the latter being mined and sunk off that port in March, 1945.

The careers of the three ships at Calais from November, 1944 can best be described separately.

Shepperton Ferry (Code No.RD347)

After further trials, the *Shepperton* began a regular service in December, 1944. The primary task was to offload locomotives to augment the much depleted stock of the French Railways, as the S.N.C.F. had lost numerous engines due to bombing. Each train ferry also caried a ramp at the stern which, when aligned with the berth, enabled vehicles to be driven on and off. This proved particularly important at the time of the Ardennes offensive in December, 1944 when the British 6th Airborne Division was sent by sea from the U.K. as a back up force. Some of the heavy transport came on the train ferries and Landing Ships Tank into Calais. The vehicles which caused most difficulty were the R.A.F. 'Queen Marys', long low slung lorries used mainly for the transport of damaged fighter aircraft. The *Shepperton* ran regularly until 12th March, when she went off for boiler cleaning. On 22nd February, 1945 I contrived to embark on her when I was going on leave as she sailed at 0800 hrs and the *Canterbury* and *Princess Maud* were not sailing until the afternoon tide. My efforts to snatch seven hours extra leave were unsuccessful, however, as we were fog-bound off Dover for several hours. None of the ships had radar at that time and, when the fog lifted, we found ourselves in the middle of a fleet of Landing Craft Tanks fortunately without mishap.

It had been agreed that the train ferries could carry up to 800 troops to help clear a backlog although this created some problems at Dover. On this occasion there was only one other passenger but the lounge under the bridge was still furnished, as was the Dining Saloon further aft used by the ship's officers.

Like the *Canterbury* the train ferries were painted grey overall at this time but, when the *Shepperton* returned from a brief refit on the Tyne in the summer of 1945, her funnels were back in Southern Railway colours though the hull was still grey.

At the end of the war the *Shepperton* and *Hampton* were employed, inter alia, on returning Army vehicles for units being moved back to

Shepperton Ferry berthed at Calais in August 1946.　　　　　　(Keith Lewis)

the U.K. including some of the transport of the 6th Airborne Division which they had brought to Calais in such haste in December, 1944. In May, 1945, however, the 6th Airborne Division were returning after their successful drop east of the Rhine in March, 1945.

Captain Sidney Kingsland remained with the *Shepperton* until he transferred to the Biarritz in the summer of 1945. The Master I recall most clearly was Captain William (Bill) J. Waters who succeeded him. Slight in stature but kindly with a warm sense of humour, we were occasionally invited to lunch on board when the *Shepperton* was delayed by weather. He in turn sometimes spent the evening ashore with us and he and Captain Payne attended the farewell party when George Wharton and I both left Calais for Germany at the same time in March, 1946. I did not see him again until October, 1964 when crossing on the *Invicta* by which time he was Senior Master. After leaving Dover, I sent my card up to the bridge with some diffidence but he came down and the years fell away immediately as we chatted for nearly an hour until he was required back on the bridge to take the ship into Calais. Bill Waters was the subject of a 'Profile' in 'The Observer' in August, 1959 and I am indebted to them for the following paragraphs.

Born in 1901, he joined the then South Eastern and Chatham Railway in 1916 as a cabin boy, becoming a deck hand on one of the cargo ships eighteen months later. He became a Master of the Southern Railway cargo ships in 1935, transferred to the Train Ferries during the war and to the passener ships later in 1946.

It is his comments in the article which really brings the man to life, however: 'It's a lovely life. I wouldn't have any other job. I remember when the school-master called me out I said exactly what I was going to do and I did it. Maybe there was a certain amount of luck attached to it. But I did it and I never regretted it'.

On the technical side: 'I've been in and out of port about 25,000 times in my career with only superficial mishaps. I don't think that's a bad reord. We come in astern at about 15 knots ready for a quick turn round. Calais and Boulogne are difficult in a North Westerly gale and a flood tide. You have to shoot the pierheads at an angle.

'This job's more nerve than anything else. If you start worrying you're lost. You must have anticipation but not too much imagination. The first thing that makes a happy ship is if the Chief Engineer and the Master get on all right. A happy ship starts from the Master. If he's a worry guts it'll soon go right through the ship.'

Finally on the personal side: 'I don't find it monotonous. I get to know people — people I'd never have a chance of meeting otherwise. At home I sometimes play chess or watch the wife gardening. I turn out at six in the morning. I hear the birds whistling (at his home above Dover) and I might be in the country. Sometimes I sit and I think. Sometimes I just sit. My greatest hobby is watching people. I can lean on my gate and watch lorry drivers. What are they thinking? How will they be when they get to the end of it? It does give me pleasure. Where are these people going in such a hurry?

'Another thing I like to watch are the gulls behind the ship, trimming their wings to the wind like sails. They can go faster then we can without moving their wings.'

Captain Waters retired in 1966 but, sadly, died in 1969.

Twickenham Ferry (Code No.RD348)

The *Twickenham* was the second merchant ship into Calais, arriving on 14th December, 1944. She had already had the distinction of being the first Southern Railway Ship into Cherbourg at the end of August, 1944.

Although all went well at first, January, 1945 cast a jinx on the ship. On 3rd January she was damaged entering Dover and out of service for three days. On the 11th she sustained damage to her lifting gear. Finally on 24th January at 1100 hrs while on passage to Calais she was in collision with the tug *Empire Rupert* which sank with the loss of ten of her crew. The *Twickenham* entered Dover at 1400 hrs assisted by the tugs *Lady Duncannon* and *Justice*. She was able to sail for Cowes on 26th January to have a new stem casing fitted at Southampton.

Early in May, 1945 she was back at Cherbourg for berthing trials for a new ramp but she returned to the Dover – Calais route on 19th May to allow the *Shepperton* to leave for her refit. After the *Shepperton*'s return she reverted to the Southampton – Cherbourg service.

The *Twickenham* was normally commanded by Captain C.A. Hancock, D.S.C., the Commodore of the Southern Railway Fleet. He retired in August, 1946.

Hampton Ferry (Code No.RD346)

The *Hampton* did not appear in Calais until mid February, 1945. Like her sister she had been running on the Southampton – Cherbourg route but was in dock for a month for overhaul and repairs prior to her arrival in Calais.

The *Hampton* had two main claims to fame during her service to Calais. In May, 1945 she unloaded the 1,000th locomotive to be shipped to the port. Secondly, on 21st October, 1945, to assist the clearance of a backlog, she carried the largest number of troops to embark on one ship — 2,350. Fortunately the weather was kind as only 800 could be accommodated on the boat deck and the remainder stood or sat on the steel plating of the train deck.

By the autumn of 1945, traffic on the Train Ferries was fairly light. A typical return load for the *Hampton* on 2nd January, 1946 consisted of eight LNER Ambulance coaches, five 2.8 locos and tenders plus three vehicles loaded with Naval stores.

The *Hampton* was commanded initially by Captain Masters before his departure to the *Biarritz* and then by Captain Waters before he switched to the *Shepperton*. Her regular Master in the winter of 1945/46 was Captain William (Bill or 'Basher') Baxter. He was another jovial, extrovert character, always ready for a chat and a joke. One day sitting in his cabin, I said I had never pulled the cord to

Hampton Ferry at sea off Stranraer in 1942.   (National Maritime Museum)

sound off a ship's whistle or siren. He told me to go ahead. But we then had to send a hasty message to the duty tug to tell them there was nothing amiss on the *Hampton*. I last saw him in 1953 when he was in command of the *Canterbury*. He retired in 1961 and died in 1967.

In March, 1946 the train ferries were derequisitioned and returned to the Southern Railway on the understanding that they would continue to carry service as well as commercial freight particularly export cargoes but no service personnel except for those accompanying freight. From this time the story of the three ships can now again be merged.

An important task fell to the *Hampton* and *Shepperton* in the late summer of 1946. At this time I was on the staff of Q (Movements) at British Army of the Rhine Headquarters at Bad Oeuynhausen. The main task was planning Operation 'UNION' i.e. the movement of married families to the Rhine Army. Personnel were shipped to Cuxhaven on the troopships *Empire Halladale* and *Empire Trooper* but the unaccompanied baggage had to be transported by another route. Mindful of the inevitable pilferage in German ports at that time of shortages, I suggested that freight waggons should be guarded by a platoon of infantry from the Stratford goods depot in East London via Dover – Calais to various West German destinations. Twelve trains were duly despatched safely on the Train Ferries.

Having completed her duties at Southampton, the *Twickenham* returned to Dover on 19th July, 1946 but, as her gantry had been

Hampton Ferry leaving Southampton for Cherbourg in 1944. N.B. Gantry for unloading in French ports. (W.H. Mitchell)

removed, she could no longer be used on the Calais service. The Southern Railway had decided that the ships, whilst refitting for peacetime service, should be converted to burn oil instead of coal. The *Shepperton* left for the Clyde in May, 1947 to join the *Twickenham* which was already in dock at Glasgow. The *Hampton* maintained the Calais service until 11th October, 1947 when it was finally closed after almost three years. The *Hampton* then sailed for conversion on the Tyne.

Back in Dover, the *Twickenham* sailed for Dunkirk on 27th October to be handed back to the French. The Dunkirk service was resumed by the *Twickenham* and *Shepperton* on 1st December, for cargo only initially due to a French strike, but the full Night Ferry service started again on 15th December, 1947, over eight years after it had been suspended. The *Hampton* joined the other two ships early in 1948.

For the next four years the three ships maintained the Dover – Dunkirk service. Late in 1951 they were joined by the new diesel-engined French *Saint Germain*. Although faster than the pre-war ships, her diesel judder did not make for peaceful sleep particularly when manoeuvring in Dunkirk locks.

The tragic loss of the *Princess Victoria* between Stranraer and Larne in January, 1953 took the *Hampton* back to that route every summer to help with vehicle and passenger traffic from 1953 to 1961. The *Shepperton* also relieved at Stranraer in the spring from 1962 to 1965.

However, by 1969 the ships were 35 years old, and the arrival in July of the new multi-purpose British Rail ship *Vortigern* enabled a start to be made with phasing them out.

By chance I was in Holyhead on 16th September, 1969 when the *Hampton* steamed rather laboriously into the outer harbour; next day she was in dry dock. She was towed from Holyhead to the Gareloch in December, having been sold to the Chandris Group though previously the Venezuelans had shown some interest. She was renamed *Tre-Arddur* and eventually left the Gareloch under tow on 29th June, 1971 arriving at Piraeus on 19th July. Her role in Greek waters is not recorded. Whatever it was, it did not last long, as she arrived at Valencia for breaking up, again under tow, on 19th July, 1973.

The *Shepperton* was withdrawn on 25th August, 1972 and went to the breakers at Bilbao on 12th September. She was still being broken up there when her wartime companion from Calais, the *Princess Maud* arrived in early 1973 for scrapping.

Due to the late delivery of the French *Saint Eloi*, the *Twickenham* sailed on until May, 1974, although by then the S.N.C.F.'s *Chartres*, primarily used as a car ferry, as was the *Vortigern*, but also a multi-purpose ship had arrived. The *Twickenham* thus achieved the unique distinction of being the last survivor of all the ships which served Calais between November, 1944 and August, 1947.

Captain John Arthur, who retired as Commodore of the entire *Sealink* (U.K.) fleet in August, 1981 should really have appeared in this story before. But, as he himself has said in print that the old Train Ferries, particularly the *Shepperton*, which he commanded from 1960 to 1961, were his favourite commands, it seems appropriate for him to feature in this chapter.

John Arthur joined the Shaw Savill and Albion Line as a cadet in 1935 and obtained his Second Officer's certificate in 1938 and his Master's certificate in 1944. Under the complex wartime rules for deck officers, he served as a Temporary Lieutenant, R.N.R., in the aircraft carrier H.M.S. *Indomitable* in 1942. 1944 found him back with Shaw Savill on their flagship the *Dominion Monarch* then

Shepperton Ferry leaving Dover in her last years.　　　　　　　　(John Hendy)

trooping on the North Atlantic. By this time he had a wife and baby in Kent and naturally wished to give up 'deep sea' voyaging. He accordingly applied successfully to join the Southern Railway and was appointed Second Officer of the *Canterbury* in January, 1945. The *Canterbury*'s gross tonnage of 3,000 compared with the 27,000 tons of the *Dominion Monarch* so not unnaturally he found the former ship rather small. The four months he spent on the *Canterbury*, however, marked the beginning of a friendship with Captain Walker which still continues after forty years. At the end of the war he transferred to the *Autocarrier* then based on Southampton but by 1946 he was back in Dover and served for a period as Second Officer on the *Biarritz* with Captain Masters. He recalls a race into Calais with the *Canterbury*, by then on the 'Golden Arrow' service. The *Biarritz* won, despite her age, though there was some suggestion that she took a short cut from the official channel.

Apart from the Train Ferries and the passenger ships, Captain Arthur commanded in turn the car ferries, *Lord Warden*, *Maid of Kent*, and *Dover*. He then spent eleven years as Master of the multi-purpose (i.e. train or car ferry) ship *Vortigern* before his final two years in command of the new flagship *St Anselm*.

106

I asked Captain Arthur if he would be willing to provide me with a technical passage on the handling of the Train Ferries. What follows represents his entire philosophy on the operation of such ships by a Captain who is acknowledged as one of the country's greatest living experts on the subject. I am proud to include this and grateful to John Arthur for writing it. I am sure, however, that he would agree with me that, despite their defects particularly in the post-war years, the three ships which form the subject of this chapter performed yeoman service in peace and war and the passing of the 'Night Ferry' service is a matter for regret.

'Before going into the various technicalities regarding the specific handling of the old pre-war train ferries there are a few general observations that are extremely relevant. Any new tonnage, especially if it is a departure from the accepted type, is suspect, and the attitude of mind, of its first Master, is of paramount importance to its future.

'It is ordinary human nature to be suspicious of the unknown, to be over confident can be as disastrous as being ultra-pessimistic, thus the correct attitude of mind towards a new ship plays a very important role as to its future, especially in the field of handling.

'My attitude was completely straight forward, deal in facts. Carefully work out what is reasonable to expect from the power of the equipment available, anticipate all manoeuvres that may need to be executed, consider all conditions and attempt to work out a system that will be effective in extreme weather conditions, it will work in normal weather.

'Ships do not go from "A" to "B" by willing them to do so. They go because the correct forces have been brought into play. If the theory of a manoeuvre is correct, but it does not appear to work, it does not make the theory wrong, it means the operator has made a mess of the theory. Remember I said "if the theory is correct".

'New ships, at their trials should be put through all their paces, forwards, backwards, sideways, swinging, stopping, breakdowns, one engine, two engines, anchors, crash stops, rudders, thrusts, the first Master must let his imagination run wild and with the aid of his Chief Engineer and Officers attempt to envisage the most bizarre situations and be prepared for every conceivable emergency. It is impossible to envisage all emergencies and manoeuvring requirements, but experience helps — there is no short cut to experience — it comes with time and right up to the end of my 48 years at sea I was well aware that there was still lots to learn. Remember, no matter what power is put into a ship, the time will come when the elements will beat you.

'Give a ship a bad name to start with and the die is set, it will take a lot to break it, if ever. The old train ferries suffered from this stigma. They were new, they were large by comparison with other tonnage of the time, they were under-powered, by a similar comparison, the fact that the other tonnage was grossly over-powered was not accepted. They unnerved many.

'I watched those old train ferries suffer, bigger and better crashes, services disrupted and to my mind it was nationalization that kept them going — no private concern could or would have accepted the damage bills. I wondered if they would survive for me to have a go. I had the very good fortune to sail, as Mate, with a certain Captain Coulter, who allowed me to handle and gave me great encouragement. He handled well and let me experiment, to a degree, as I was certain there were many manoeuvres which needed to be evaluated. Shore based Marine Superintendents do not like departures from accepted procedures, are generally conservative in their outlook and the longer ashore the less they know of the practicabilities of ship handling.

'It was 1960, I was Master of the *Shepperton Ferry*. That summer we were stand-by ship, one crew only. I was in sole Command. We fitted in, in between regular services, as requisite. Now was my opportunity to try out my theories.

'In those days the Western Entrance to Dover harbour was blocked. The time honoured method of arriving at the Ferry Dock stern first, was to enter the Eastern Entrance, with the end of the Eastern Arm in line with the Prince of Wales Pier light, swing 180 degrees to starboard, proceed stern first across the harbour, 90 degrees to starboard round the Prince of Wales Pier and then straight down to the ferry dock. Had I been in a ship bound for the Camber, at the eastern end of the harbour, I would have swung 90 degrees to port, after entering and then proceeded stern first into Camber. Why should I do this 180 degree swing to starboard, better, surely, to cross the harbour head first, swing 90 degrees to port and then stern first into the ferry dock. The obvious benefit, head first across the harbour and cut out 180 degree swing. I tried it, it worked perfectly, the Manager and Marine Superintendent questioned me as to what I was up to; I believe the Manager accepted my actions, but not so the Marine Superintendent — "well it's up to you, but don't expect me to support you if you come unstuck". Then it was "what about tide time?", when there was a strong set into No.5 berth, Admiralty Pier. Here again the tide helped the swing to port, in fact on one or two occasions, in nice calm weather, I did the swing without using the engines. It also proved a great advantage in all weather conditions. However when the Western Entrance was cleared, I was forbidden to do this particular swing, was called before the Manager, and had to apologise to the Dover Harbour Master, but I am glad to say that a change of management, both in ours and Dover Harbour Board, and we were back to a proper seaman-like manoeuvre.

'I carried on with my theories and experiments. The understanding of Newton's laws of motion, kinetic energy and the parallelogram of forces are the key to successful ship handling and the days of rubbing one's favourite charm, reputed to be a rabbit's paw in the old days at Folkestone, were gone as far as I was concerned, not that I had ever given them any consideration. I was convinced that careful thought of all the forces which affect manoeuvring and experimenting in quiet conditions was the key to success with these, so called, low powered ships. The anchor gear was absolutely first class in those old train ferries and I evolved a system of using the anchor, instead of a tug, to hold the bow whilst berthing. Years later this anchor drill proved its worth — in eleven years with the *Vortigern* I never used a tug whilst on service in Dover, and the same applied to my last Command M.V. *St Anselm* which I brought out new in October, 1980 and retired from in August, 1981.

'Actual speed is hard to assess until passing close to an object and so it is when making the Ferry Dock, it is not until you are passing the jetty that you can assess the speed to any accurate degree. My yardstick was by the berthing crew, who were standing by to take my lines, if they merely had to walk to keep up with me I was going too slow, however if they had to run I was going too fast and that is very dangerous on entry into that dock. The water is pushed into the dock and builds up a wall of water which has the effect of slowing the vessel's sternway, but as the vessel slows down the water rushes out down the sides of the ship and out into the harbour leaving a void astern into which the ship will now accelerate and great care must be exercised to make sure that induced sternway is counteracted by a good ahead move on the engines.

'To handle the old train ferries needed the correct seaman-like approach, appreciation of wind and tidal conditions, utilization of the movement of the vessel, then by using the power of kinetic energy, the correct positioning before making a berth anticipating engine moves well in advance and to be sure they were ticking over in the right direction before applying a heavy move and last, but not least a good relationship with the Chief Engineer who, should you get into an emergency situation, could well prove to be your best friend.

'To me they were a challenge, I got the opportunity to experiment and am pleased to observe, years later, many of my manoeuvres being accepted in our new and more sophisticated ships. So finally let me take you, on the old *Shepperton Ferry*, into the ferry dock with a stiff breeze off the jetty. Short swing off the end of the Prince of Wales Pier, full astern, about half way through the swing the wind pushes the bow to the east, the stern clears the Prince of Wales Pier, the ferry dock is open, that means I can see the east side of the jetty, the vessel is starting to pick up sternway, bow rudder hard a starboard, but not yet effective, the end of the jetty is lost from the starboard wing of the bridge, ease the port engine, looking down I see the astern wash passing below me, the bow rudder will now become effective, back to full astern port, the QM has got the vessel on the rudder. "Let her come to the middle of the jetty, steady". I am now driving the vessel to windward, she is travelling, the old ferries had about three quarters of their ahead speed astern, around 14 knots, stop both. The movement of the ship is taking us in, just inside the end of the jetty, the shore force are running, slow ahead to get the engines turning in the right direction. "Right down the middle QM." I need the speed otherwise the old girl would drop to leeward and the stern could miss the hole, or the port quarter take a knock, just to be sure increase the starboard engine to full ahead, then back to slow ahead both. The stern has entered she is running true, but now slowing up because of the build up of water astern. Now is the time to watch very carefully, the water is rushing past me under the bridge and now we are gathering sternway, time to hold the old girl, increase to full ahead, but don't keep it on too long or you will be going out of the dock, that's it, stop, half ahead starboard to keep the port quarter off the tapper of the dock astern where it runs into the shoe and make absolutely sure that the stern does not bump into the shoe. Two feet to go to the bridge mark, stop, the lines are fast, ring off main engines, she's there, came in like a rat up a drain pipe, no tug, no bumps, well done all, instant job satisfaction.'

Chapter 18
Other Ships

A The Mail Coasters

As recorded in Chapter 2, priority was given, inter alia, to the reconstruction of the Quai Paul Devot. The Quai was ready by 15th February, 1945. This enabled what became known as the 'Mail Coaster'
service to commence. This played a most important part in
maintaining Army morale and the 'mail train' which ran initially to
Belgium and the Netherlands, was extended to the British Zone of
Germany at the end of the war calling at Munster, Hanover and
Hamburg. This was further extended to Neumunster in July, 1945.

Between 1924 and 1928 the Southern Railway built nine cargo
vessels between 700 and 800 tons to serve in the Straits and from
Southampton to the Channel Islands. Those built for the Straits' service were *Hythe* and *Whitstable* (1925), *Maidstone* (1926) and *Deal*
(1928), together with *Tonbridge* and *Minster*, both lost in the war.
The ships built specifically for the Channel Islands were *Haslemere*,
Ringwood and *Fratton* (also lost in the war). The ships were all built
by D.W. Henderson & Co. Ltd of Glasgow and although primarily
intended for cargo, including cattle, some carried up to twelve
passengers.

Although, after the war, there were some variations in routes, this
chapter is concerned with *Hythe, Maidstone* and *Deal*.

Hythe

Hythe was present at Dunkirk as a transport commanded by Captain
W. Baxter, (see *Hampton Ferry*) and brought back 674 men on 31st
May, 1940. She first arrived in Calais in February, 1945 when the
Quai Paul Devot was ready to receive ships. Apart from Army Mail
she also carried cargo for the Military Forwarding Organization
(M.F.O.). This Army title was an all embracing one covering all
unaccompanied baggage or small items of cargo which did not fit
into the normal bulk cargo schedule. Such cargo was strictly supervised and documented to prevent theft and the service through Calais

111

Hythe off Dover. (National Railway Museum)

continued for a long period though Hamburg became the main centre for Rhine Army.

During the four month period from May to August, 1945 the mail coasters discharged 7,942 tons of Army mail and loaded 2,173 tons. This may not sound large in terms of tonnage but mail is, of course, a light, bulky cargo.

The *Hythe* was handed back to the Southern Railway by the Ministry of Transport in August, 1945 but continued to give priority to Army cargoes. She re-opened the Boulogne Services in March, 1946 under the command of Captain Gartside, formerly Chief Officer of the *Canterbury*. This was to be her permanent route, mainly from Folkestone until she was broken up in 1956 in Dover.

Maidstone

Maidstone was the second ship to operate the mail coaster service. She had served during the war, as had *Deal* under the White Ensign, as a balloon barrage ship, based on Sheerness, until May, 1943, under the name *Bungay* to avoid confusion with the depot ship H.M.S. *Maidstone*. After this she was based on Stranraer for a period before returning to the Straits at the end of the war. She ran in tandem with *Hythe* carrying mail, M.F.O. traffic and other cargo. This continued until November, 1946 when she had a lengthy refit at Newhaven which included the conversion of the space previously used for horses to accommodation for the crew. Much fumigation must have been required. She apparently carried twelve passengers at this time. She transferred to the Heysham – Belfast route in 1953 and remained on this service until 1958. On 14th December of that year she was towed to Antwerp to be broken up.

Deal

Deal, the last of the nine ships to be built, had a varied wartime career. After her release by the Royal Navy, she operated from Fishguard to Cork in November, 1943. February, 1944 found her on the Manchester – Belfast route and subsequently running from Heysham to Belfast.

The liberation of the Channel Islands, however, caused another move as wartime losses had resulted in a shortage of ships. She served that route until November, 1945 but ran regularly to Calais after *Hythe* was transferred to Boulogne.

From mid 1947 she too ran mainly to Boulogne. After 1958 she was the sole survivor of the ships, which had used the inner tidal berth at Folkestone. She was withdrawn in February, 1963 and broken up at Ghent.

B Landing Craft

LANDING SHIPS TANK (LSTs)

Although the hards built at the landward end of the Avant Port could receive all types of Landing Craft, they were only used for LSTs right at the beginning, i.e. at the end of December, 1944 at the time of the Ardennes offensive. After this Ostend and Antwerp coped with these vessels. Since they carried so many more vehicles than the smaller types of landing craft, it was sensible to offload them as near to the front as possible. There were, however, some losses of LSTs en route to both Ostend and Antwerp due to enemy action while the war lasted.

LANDING CRAFT TANK (Lcts)

Calais was, however, utilized on a regular basis for Landing Craft Tank for two periods. A flotilla ran from Dover from 25th January to 10th March, 1945 when the service was switched to Tilbury – Ostend. Another flotilla, which had previously run to Boulogne, operated from 2nd May to 31st July, 1945. During this second period the total shipments were:

	In	Out
Vehicles	4,795	2,267
Personnel	3,895	3,044

The outward total in May included 1,072 vehicles and 1,840 personnel of 6th Airborne Division and 1st Mountain Regiment Royal Artillery shipped on LCTs and the Train Ferries.

C Stores Ships

A small number of supply ships with military cargoes were able to berth at the Bassin de l'Ouest in the spring of 1945. But the berths here and more particularly in the Bassin Carnot (see Chapter 3) were repaired primarily for French cargo traffic and therefore fall outside the scope of this book.

Conclusion

Today, when all the passenger ships serving Calais are primarily vehicle carriers, it is appropriate to recall the time over forty years ago when so many classic cross channel ships and the train ferries were on the Calais run.

Only three of the ships — *Canterbury, Invicta* and *Royal Daffodil* — ever visited Calais again.

Bibliography

'The Canterbury Remembered'   H. Maxwell
                                Spottiswoode, Ballantyne & Co.,
                                1970
'Steamers of British Railways' Paul Clegg & John Styring
                                T. Stephenson & Sons Ltd, 1962
'British Nationalized Shipping' Paul Clegg & John Styring
                                David & Charles, 1969
'The Short Sea Route'   Fraser G. MacHaffie
                                T. Stephenson & Sons Ltd, 1975
'Island Lifeline'   Connery Chappell
                                T. Stephenson & Sons Ltd, 1980
'Dunkirk'   A.D. Divine
                                Faber & Faber Ltd, 1945
'The Flames of Calais'   Airey Neave
                                Hodder & Stoughton, 1972
'Newhaven – Dieppe'   B.M.E. O'Mahonery, 1980

Various articles in 'Sea Breezes' and 'Ships Monthly'. Article in 'The Observer'.

FLEET LIST

Ship & Company	Date Built	Builders	Length o.a.	Breadth	Draught	Gross Tonnage	Speed Knots	Remarks
1. Southern Railway								
(a)								
Canterbury	1929	William Denny	341' 6"	47'	12' 10"	3,071	22	Scrapped 1965
Biarritz	1915	& Bros	341' 3"	45'	12' 8"	2,495	23	Scrapped 1949
Invicta	1940	,,	348'	52' 3"	12' 9"	4,178	22	Scrapped 1972
Dinard	1924	,,	325'	41'	12' 6"	2,291	19.5	Sold 1959 as *Viking*
Isle of Guernsey	1930	,,	306'	42'	12' 6"	2,143	19.5	Scrapped 1973
(b) Train Ferries								
Hampton Ferry	1934	Swan Hunter & Wigham Richardson	360'	62' 10"	12' 6"	2,989	16.5	Scrapped 1961
								Sold 1969 as *Tre-Arddur* Scrapped 1973
Shepperton Ferry	1934	,,	360'	62' 10"	12' 6"	2,996	16.5	Scrapped 1972
Twickenham Ferry	1934	,,	360'	62' 10"	12' 6"	2,839	16.5	Scrapped 1974 Owned by ALA pre & post war
(c) Mail Coasters								
Hythe	1925	D & W Henderson Glasgow	220' 6"	33' 6"	10' 6"	685	15	Scrapped 1956
Maidstone	1926	,,	220' 5"	33' 6"	10' 6"	688	15	Scrapped 1958
Deal	1928	,,	220' 5"	33' 6"	10' 6"	688	15	Scrapped 1963
2. London, Midland & Scottish Railway								
Princess Maud	1934	William Denny & Bros	330'	40' 1"	11' 6"	2,893	20	Sold 1965 as *Venus*, 1969 *Nibo*, scrapped 1973

3. Isle of Man Steam Packet Co., Ltd								
Lady of Mann	1930	Vickers, Armstrong Barrow	360'	50'	13'	3,104	23	Scrapped 1971
Ben-My-Chree	1927	Cammell Laird	355'	46'	13'	2,586	23	Scrapped 1965
Victoria	1907	William Denny & Bros	311'	40'	13'10"	1,641	21	Scrapped 1957
Manxman	1904	Vickers Sons & Maxim Barrow	330'	43'	13'6"	2,030	21	Scrapped 1949
4. General Steam Navigation Co., Ltd								
Royal Daffodil	1939	William Denny & Bros	313'	54'	8'9"	2,061	21	Scrapped 1967
5. Burns & Laird Lines Ltd								
Laird's Isle	1911	William Denny & Bros	316'	41'	14'2"	1,939	22	Scrapped 1957
6. Belgian Marine Administration								
Prinses Astrid	1929	Cockerills Hoboken	347'	46'2"	13'6"	3,088	23.5	Sunk by mine 1949
Prince Charles	1930	,,	347'	46'2"	13'6"	3,088	23.5	Scrapped 1960
Princesse Josephine Charlotte	1930	,,	347'	46'2"	13'6"	3,088	23.5	Scrapped 1950

Meresborough Books

17 Station Road, Rainham, Gillingham, Kent. ME8 7RS
Telephone: Medway (0634) 388812

We are a specialist publisher of books about Kent. Our books are available in most bookshops in the county, including our own at this address. Alternatively you may order direct, adding 10% for post (minimum 20p, orders over £20 post free). ISBN prefix 0 905270 for 3 figure numbers, 094819 for 4 figure numbers. Titles in print July 1989.

BYGONE KENT. A monthly journal on all aspects of Kent history founded October 1979. £1.50 per month. Annual Subscription £16.50 (£24.00 overseas). All back numbers available, although some only in photocopy form.

HARDBACKS

EDWARDIAN CHISLEHURST by Arthur Battle. ISBN 3433. £9.95.

FISHERMEN OF THE KENTISH SHORE by Derek Coombe. ISBN 3409 due August.

THE GILLS by Tony Conway. ISBN 266. £5.95. **BARGAIN OFFER £1.95.**

JUST OFF THE SWALE by Don Sattin. ISBN 045. £5.95.

KENT CASTLES by John Guy. ISBN 150. £7.50.

KENT'S OWN by Robin J. Brooks. The history of 500 (County of Kent) Squadron of the R.A.A.F. ISBN 541. £5.95.

LIFE AND TIMES OF THE EAST KENT CRITIC by Derrick Molock. ISBN 3077. **BARGAIN OFFER £1.95.**

THE LONDON, CHATHAM & DOVER RAILWAY by Adrian Gray. ISBN 886. £7.95.

THE NATURAL HISTORY OF ROMNEY MARSH by Dr F.M. Firth, M.A., Ph.D. ISBN 789. £6.95.

A NEW DICTIONARY OF KENT DIALECT by Alan Major. ISBN 274. £7.50.

O FAMOUS KENT by Eric Swain. ISBN 738. £9.95. **BARGAIN OFFER £4.95.**

THE PAST GLORY OF MILTON CREEK by Alan Cordell and Leslie Williams. ISBN 3042. £9.95.

THE PLACE NAMES OF KENT by Judith Glover. A comprehensive reference work. ISBN 614. Reprint due July

ROCHESTER FROM OLD PHOTOGRAPHS compiled by the City of Rochester Society. Large format. ISBN 975. £7.95. (Also available in paperback ISBN 983. £4.95.)

SHERLOCK HOLMES AND THE KENT RAILWAYS by Kelvin Jones. ISBN 3255. £8.95.

SOUTH EAST BRITAIN: ETERNAL BATTLEGROUND by Gregory Blaxland. A military history. ISBN 444. £5.95.

STRATFORD HOUSE SCHOOL 1912-1987 by Susan Pittman. ISBN 3212. £10.00.

TALES OF VICTORIAN HEADCORN or The Oddities of Heddington by Penelope Rivers (Ellen M. Poole). ISBN 3050. £8.95. (Also available in paperback ISBN 3069. £3.95.)

TEYNHAM MANOR AND HUNDRED (798-1935) by Elizabeth Selby, MBE. ISBN 630. £5.95.

TROOPSHIP TO CALAIS by Derek Spiers. ISBN 3395 due August.

TWO HALVES OF A LIFE by Doctor Kary Pole. ISBN 509. £5.95.

US BARGEMEN by A.S. Bennett. ISBN 207. £6.95.

A VIEW OF CHRIST'S COLLEGE, BLACKHEATH by A.E.O. Crombie, B.A. ISBN 223. £6.95.

STANDARD SIZE PAPERBACKS

BIRDS OF KENT: A Review of their Status and Distribution by the Kent Ornithological Society. ISBN 800. £6.95.
BIRDWATCHING IN KENT by Don Taylor. ISBN 932. £4.50.
THE CANTERBURY MONSTERS by John H. Vaux. ISBN 3441. £2.50. Due August.
THE CHATHAM DOCKYARD STORY by Philip MacDougall. ISBN 3301. £6.95.
CHIDDINGSTONE — AN HISTORICAL EXPLORATION by Jill Newton. ISBN 940. £1.95.
A CHRONOLOGY OF ROCHESTER by Brenda Purle. ISBN 851. £1.50.
COBHAM. Published for Cobham Parish Council. ISBN 3123. £1.00.
CRIME AND CRIMINALS IN VICTORIAN KENT by Adrian Gray. ISBN 967. £3.95.
CURIOUS KENT by John Vigar. ISBN 878. £1.95.
CYCLE TOURS OF KENT by John Guy. No. 1: Medway, Gravesend, Sittingbourne and Sheppey. ISBN 517. £1.50.
DOVER REMEMBERED by Jessie Elizabeth Vine. ISBN 819. £3.95.
EXPLORING KENT CHURCHES by John E. Vigar. ISBN 3018. £3.95.
EXPLORING SUSSEX CHURCHES by John E. Vigar. ISBN 3093. £3.95.
FLIGHT IN KENT. ISBN 3085. £1.95.
FROM MOTHS TO MERLINS: The History of West Malling Airfield by Robin J. Brooks. ISBN 3239. £4.95.
THE GHOSTS OF KENT by Peter Underwood. ISBN 86X. £3.95.
A HISTORY OF CHATHAM GRAMMAR SCHOOL FOR GIRLS, 1907-1982 by Audrey Perkyns. ISBN 576. £1.95.
KENT AIRFIELDS IN THE BATTLE OF BRITAIN by the Kent Aviation Historical Research Society. ISBN 3247. £4.95.
KENT COUNTRY CHURCHES by James Antony Syms. ISBN 3131. £4.50.
KENT COUNTRY CHURCHES CONTINUED by James Antony Syms. ISBN 314X. £5.95.
KENT COUNTRY CHURCHES CONCLUDED by James Antony Syms. ISBN 345X. £5.95.
KENT INNS AND SIGNS by Michael David Mirams. ISBN 3182. £3.95.
LET'S EXPLORE THE RIVER DARENT by Frederick Wood. ISBN 770. £1.95.
LULLINGSTONE PARK: THE EVOLUTION OF A MEDIAEVAL DEER PARK by Susan Pittman. ISBN 703. £3.95.
PENINSULA ROUND (The Hoo Peninsula) by Des Worsdale. ISBN 568. £1.50.
PRELUDE TO WAR by the Kent Aviation Historical Society. ISBN 3476. £2.50. Due August.
REAL ALE PUBS IN KENT by CAMRA in Kent. ISBN 3263. Was £1.95. Now 95p.
SAINT ANDREW'S CHURCH, DEAL by Gregory Holyoake. ISBN 835. 95p.
SHORNE: The History of a Kentish Village by A.F. Allen. ISBN 3204. £4.95.
SIR GARRARD TYRWHITT-DRAKE AND THE COBTREE ESTATE, MAIDSTONE by Elizabeth Melling B.A. ISBN 3344. £1.50.
SITTINGBOURNE & KEMSLEY LIGHT RAILWAY STOCKBOOK AND GUIDE. ISBN 843. 95p.
STEAM IN MY FAMILY by John Newton. ISBN 3417. £4.95.
STOUR VALLEY WALKS from Canterbury to Sandwich by Christopher Donaldson. ISBN 991. £1.95.
TALES OF VICTORIAN HEADCORN — see under hardbacks.
WADHURST: Town of the High Weald by Alan Savidge and Oliver Mason. ISBN 3352. £5.95.
WHERE NO FLOWERS GROW by George Glazebrook. ISBN 3379. £2.50.
WHO'S BURIED WHERE IN KENT by Alan Major. ISBN 3484. £4.95. Due August.
THE WORKHOUSE AND THE WEALD by Dorothy Hatcher. ISBN 3360. £4.95.

LARGE FORMAT PICTORIAL PAPERBACKS

ARE YOU BEING SERVED, MADAM? by Molly Proctor. ISBN 3174. £3.50.
AVIATION IN KENT by Robin J. Brooks. ISBN 681. £2.95.
BEFORE AND AFTER THE HURRICANE IN AND AROUND CANTERBURY by Paul Crampton. ISBN 3387. £3.50.
THE BLITZ OF CANTERBURY by Paul Crampton. ISBN 3441. £9.95.
EAST KENT FROM THE AIR by John Guy. ISBN 3158. £3.50.
EAST SUSSEX RAILWAYS IN OLD POSTCARDS by Kevin Robertson. ISBN 3220. £3.50.
GEORGE BARGEBRICK Esq. by Richard-Hugh Perks. ISBN 479. £4.50.
GOUDHURST: A Pictorial History by John T. Wilson, M.A. ISBN 3026. £2.95.
HEADCORN: A Pictorial History by the Headcorn Local History Society. ISBN 3271. £3.50.
KENT TOWN CRAFTS by Richard Filmer. ISBN 584. £2.95.
THE LIFE AND ART OF ONE MAN by Dudley Pout. ISBN 525. £2.95.
MORE PICTURES OF RAINHAM by Barbara Mackay Miller. ISBN 3298. £3.50.
THE MOTOR BUS SERVICES OF KENT AND EAST SUSSEX — A brief history by Eric Baldock. ISBN 959. £4.95.
OLD BROADSTAIRS by Michael David Mirams. ISBN 3115. £3.50.
OLD CHATHAM: A THIRD PICTURE BOOK by Philip MacDougall. ISBN 3190. £3.50.
OLD FAVERSHAM by Arthur Percival. ISBN 3425. £3.50.
OLD GILLINGHAM by Philip MacDougall. ISBN 3328. £3.50.
OLD MAIDSTONE'S PUBLIC HOUSES by Irene Hales. ISBN 533. £2.95.
OLD MAIDSTONE Vol.2 by Irene Hales. ISBN 38X. £2.50.
OLD MAIDSTONE Vol.3 by Irene Hales. ISBN 3336. £3.50.
OLD MARGATE by Michael David Mirams. ISBN 851. £3.50.
OLD PUBS OF TUNBRIDGE WELLS & DISTRICT by Keith Hetherington and Alun Griffiths. ISBN 300X. £3.50.
OLD SANDWICH by Julian Arnold and Andrew Aubertin. ISBN 673. £2.95.
OLD TONBRIDGE by Don Skinner. ISBN 398. £2.50.
PEMBURY IN THE PAST by Mary Standen. ISBN 916. £2.95.
A PICTORIAL STUDY OF ALKHAM PARISH by Susan Lees and Roy Humphreys. ISBN 3034. £2.95.
A PICTORIAL STUDY OF HAWKINGE PARISH by Roy Humphreys. ISBN 328X. £3.50.
A PICTUREBOOK OF OLD RAINHAM by Barbara Mackay Miller. ISBN 606. £3.50.
REMINISCENCES OF OLD CRANBROOK by Joe Woodwock. ISBN 331X. £3.50.
ROCHESTER FROM OLD PHOTOGRAPHS — see under hardbacks.
THOMAS SIDNEY COOPER OF CANTERBURY by Brian Stewart. ISBN 762. £2.95.
WEST KENT FROM THE AIR by John Guy. ISBN 3166. £3.50.